HAPPY EASTER

Activity Book

FOR KIDS

THiS

Coloring Book Belongs To:

_____

_____

_____

Color Test Pages

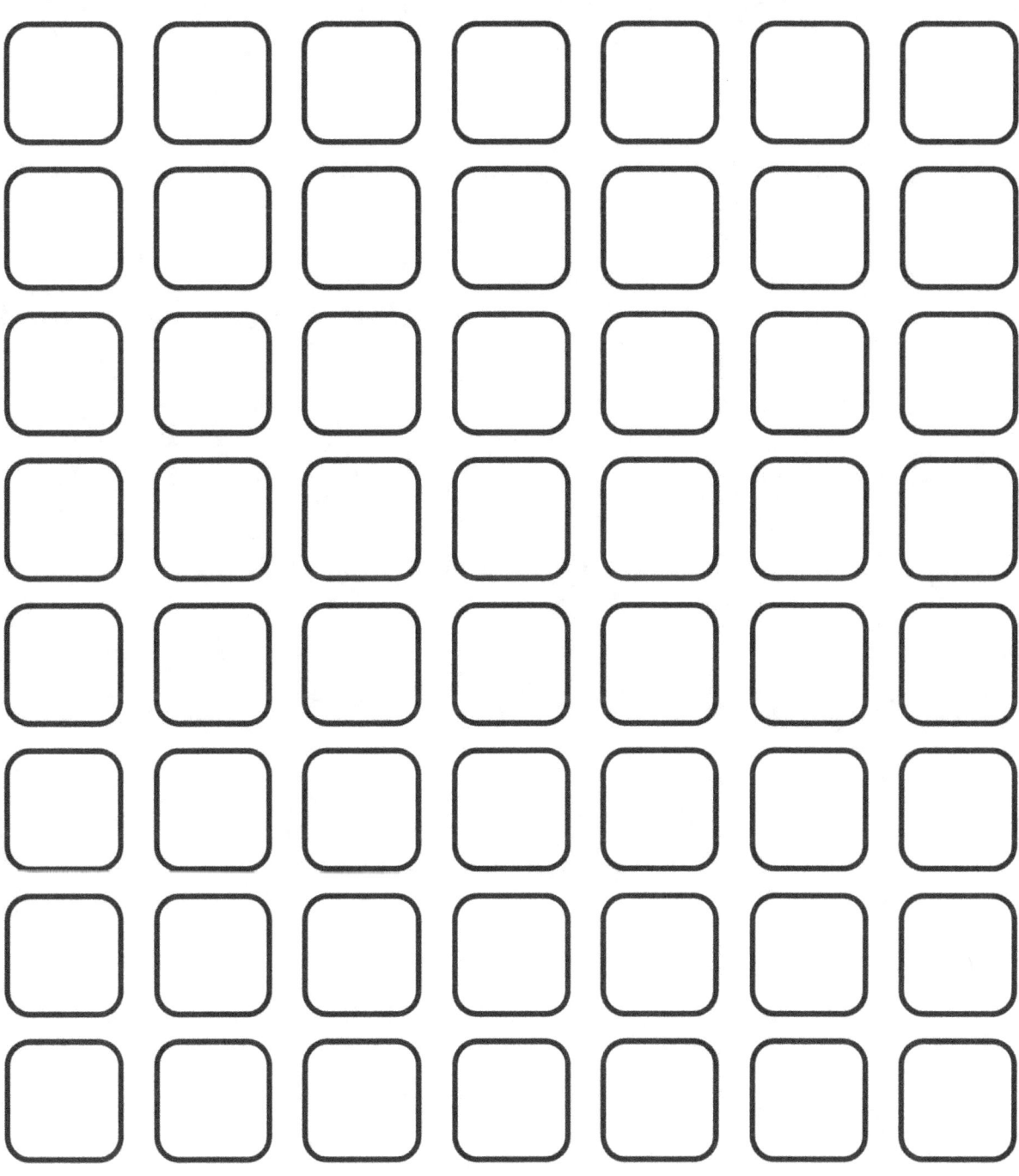

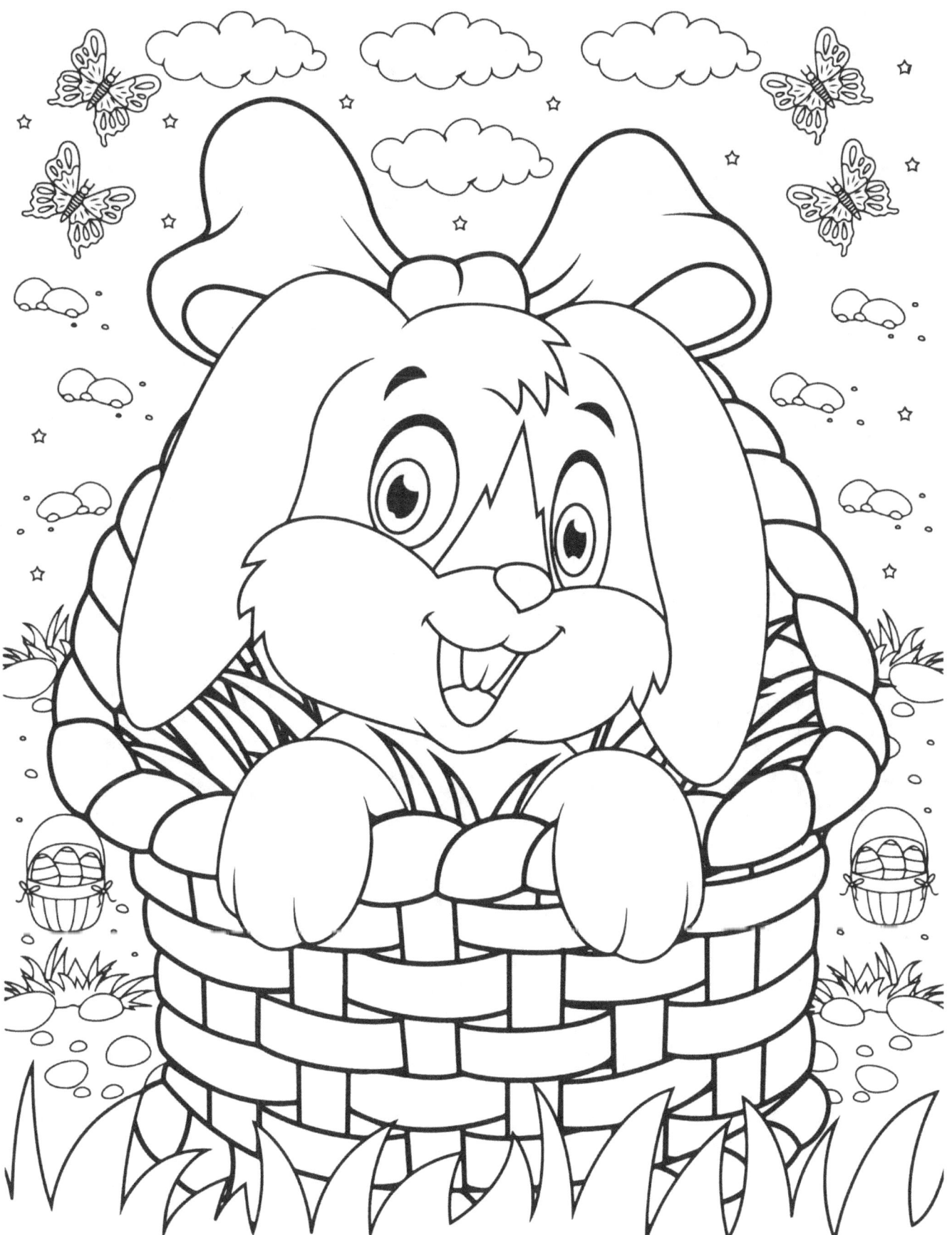

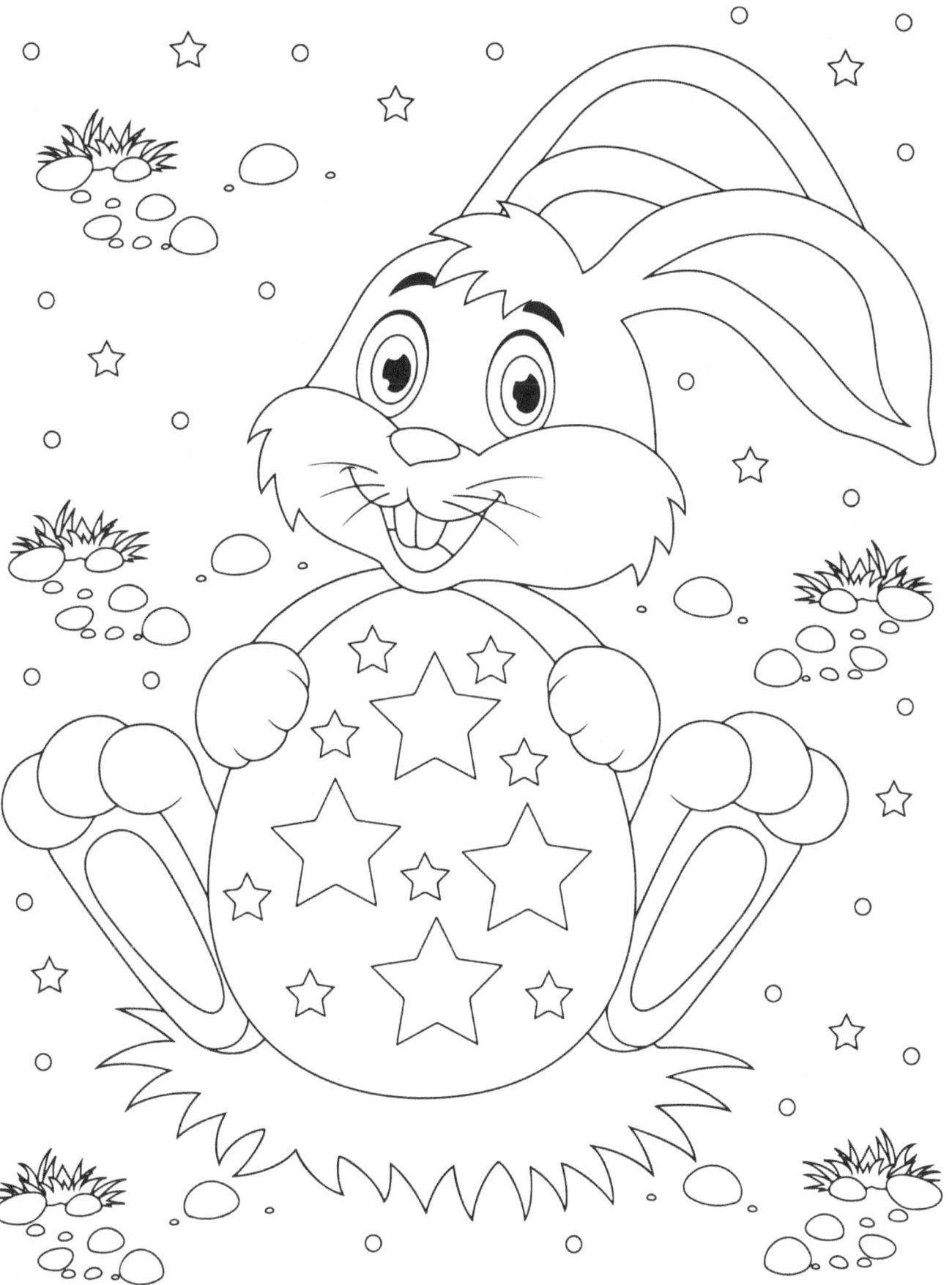

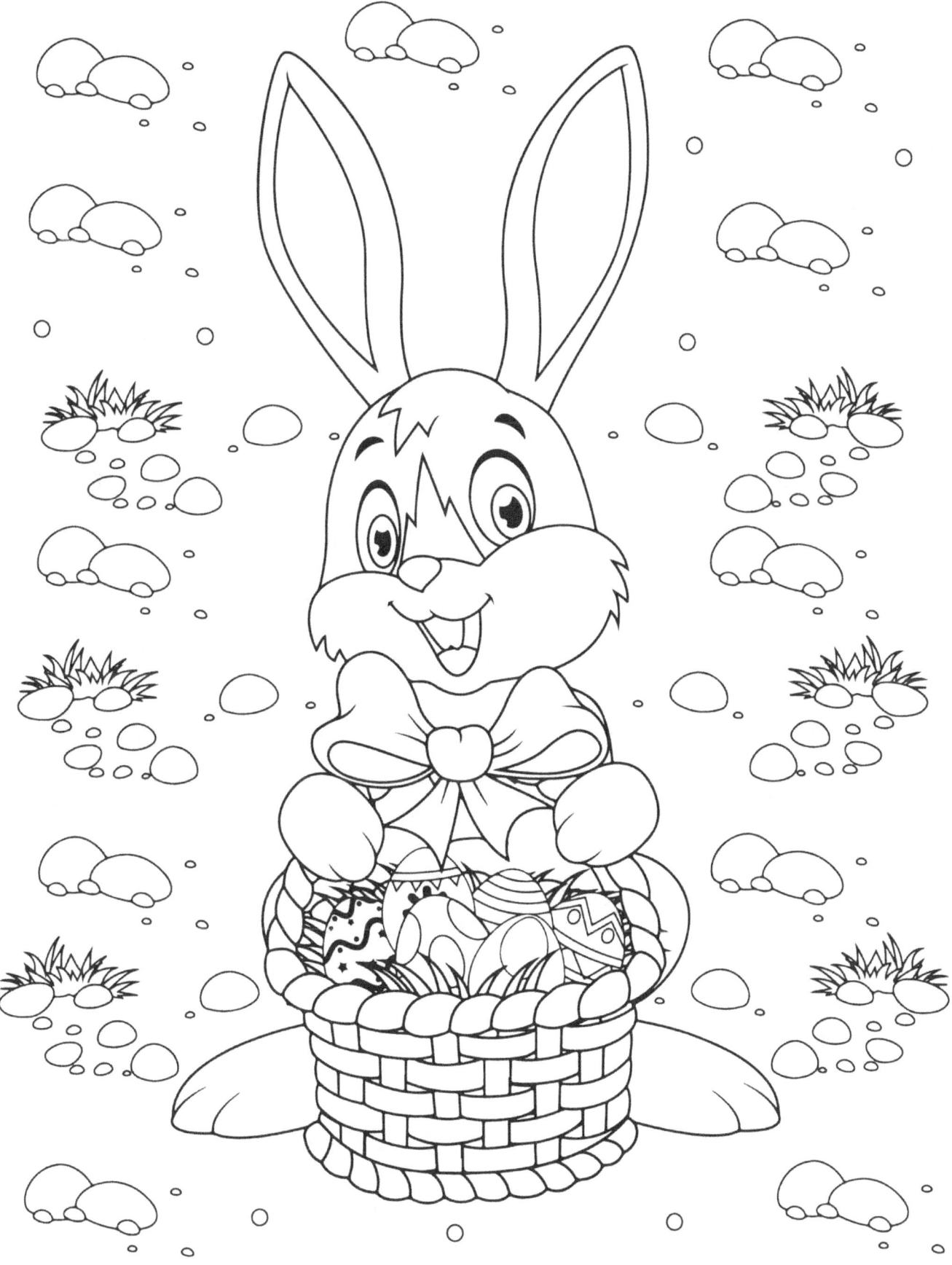

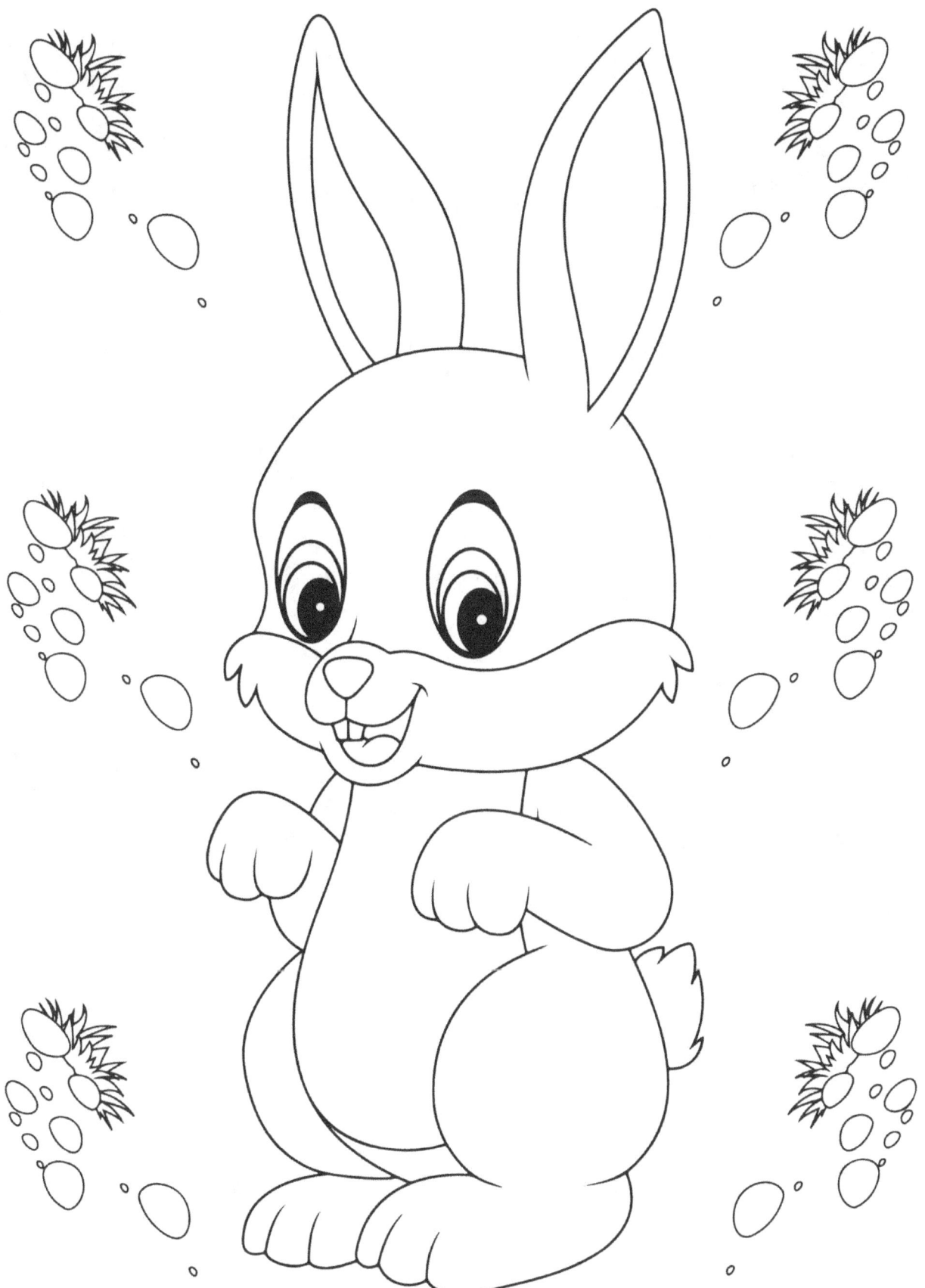

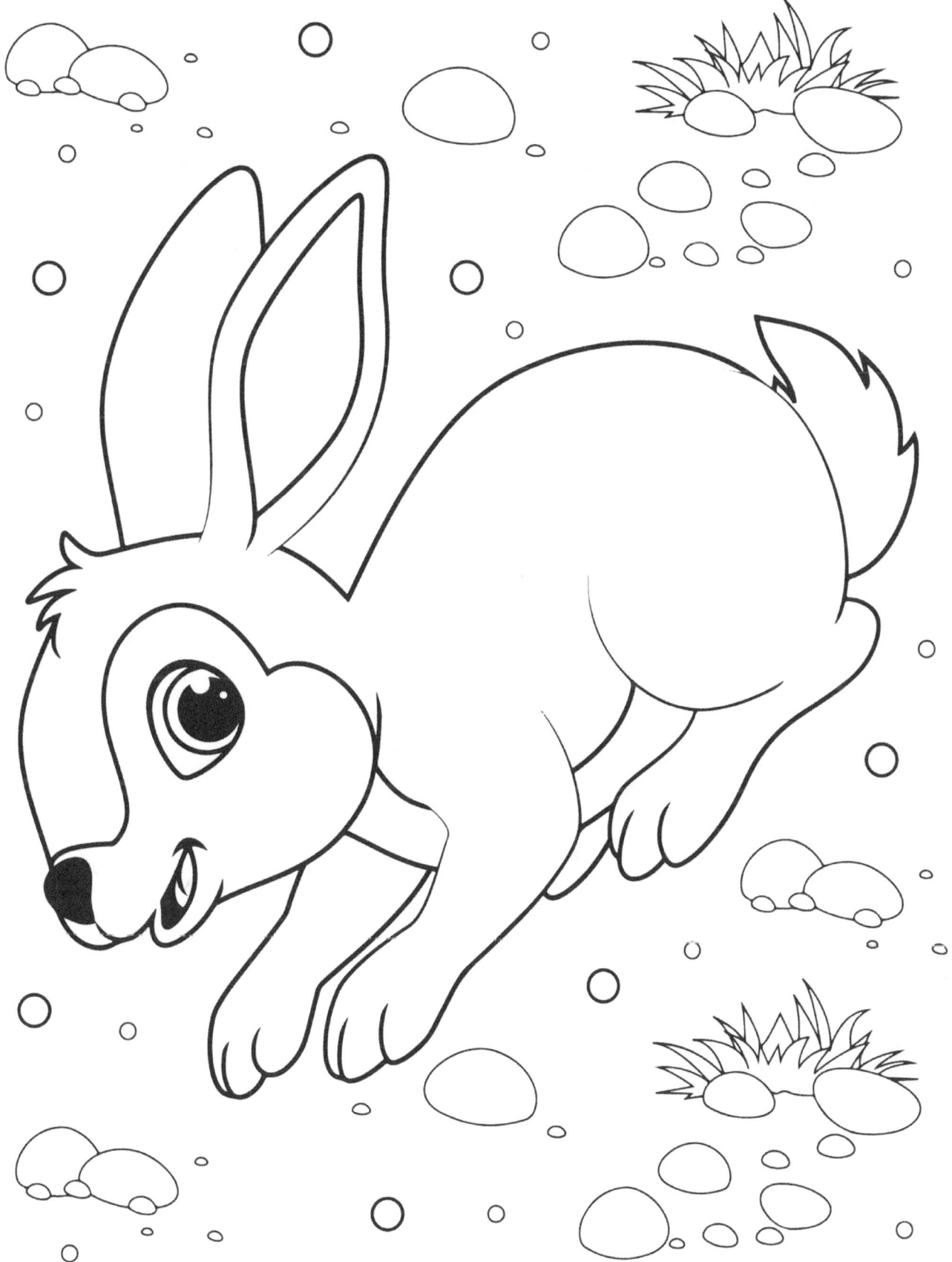

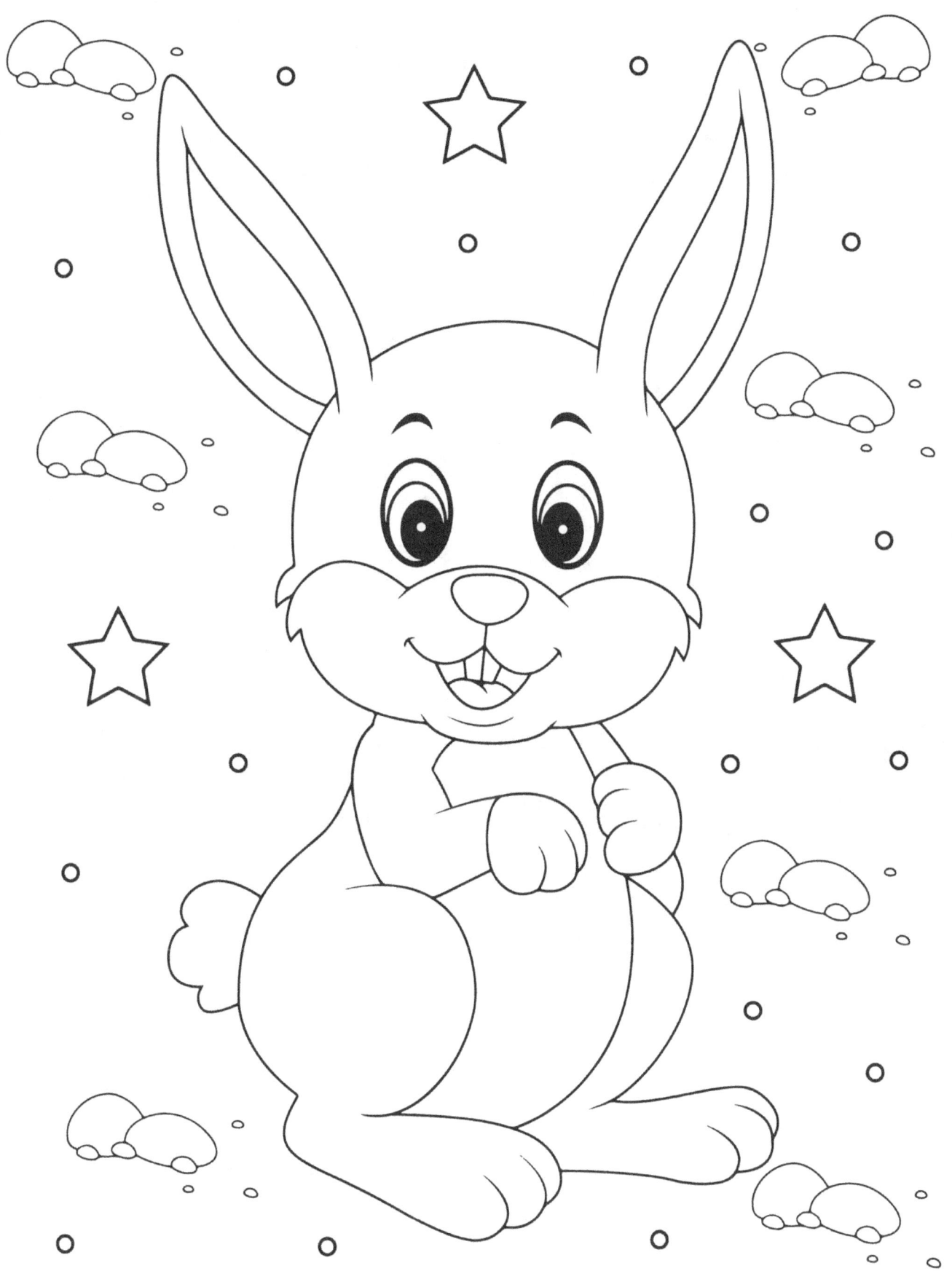

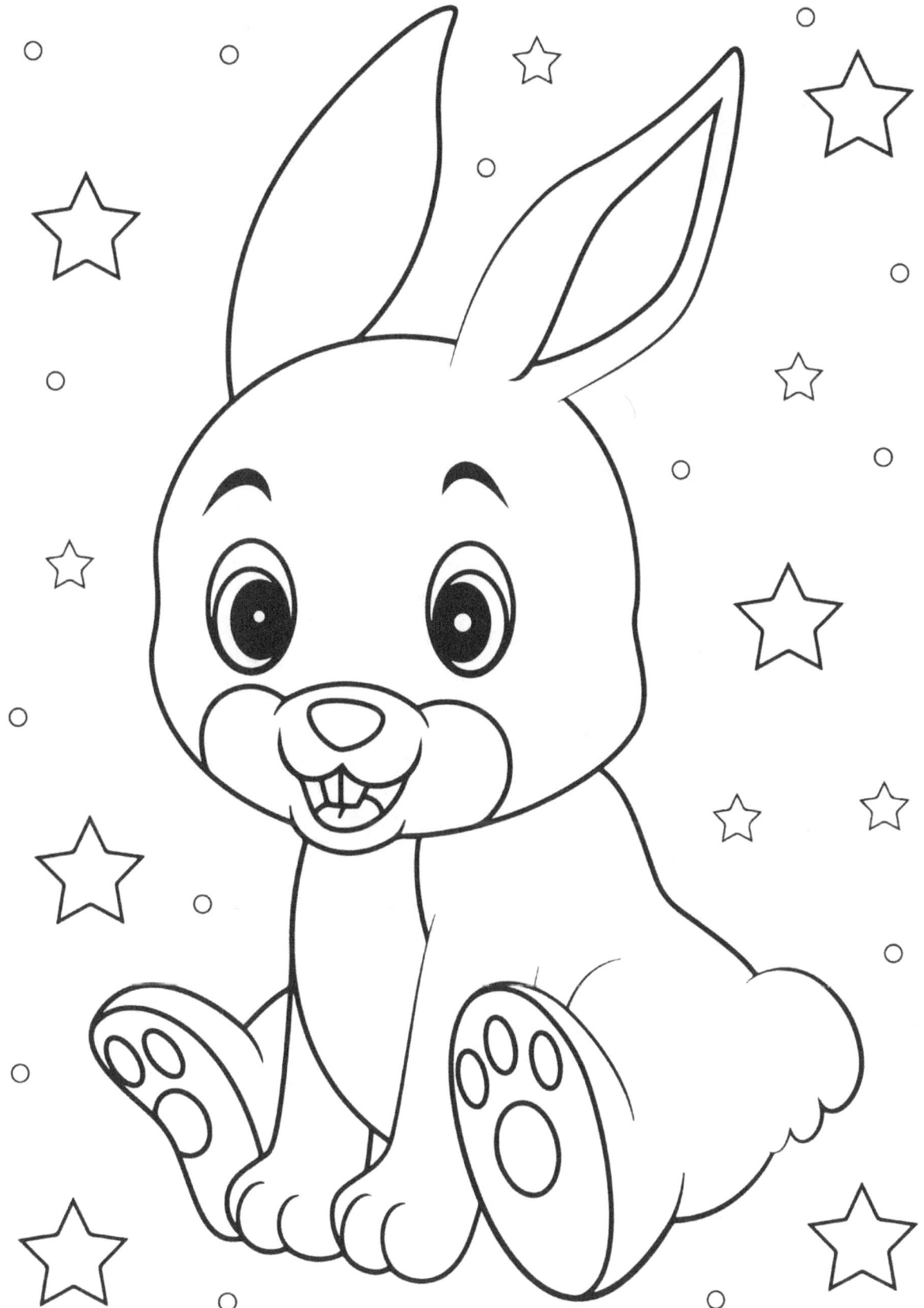

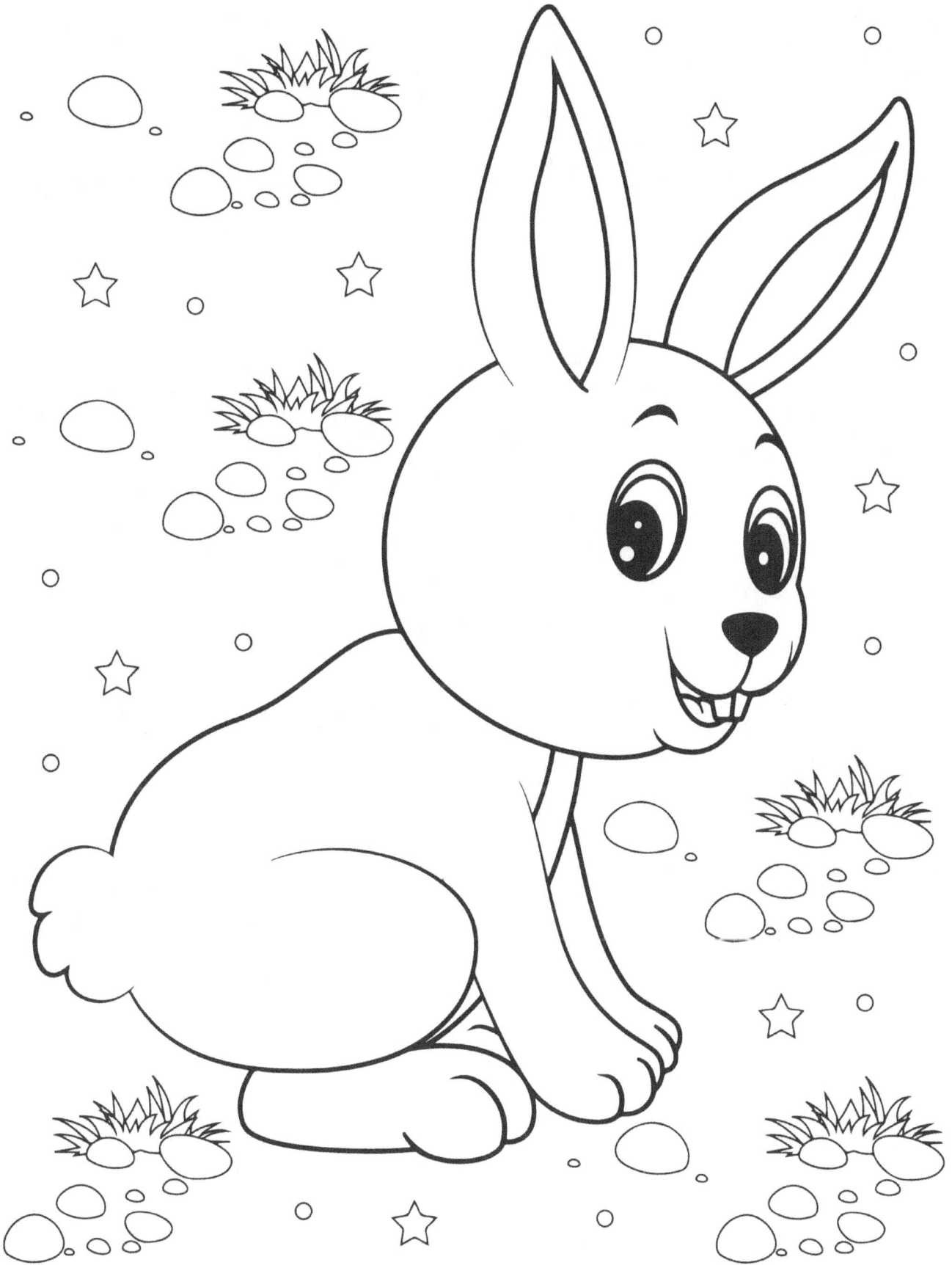

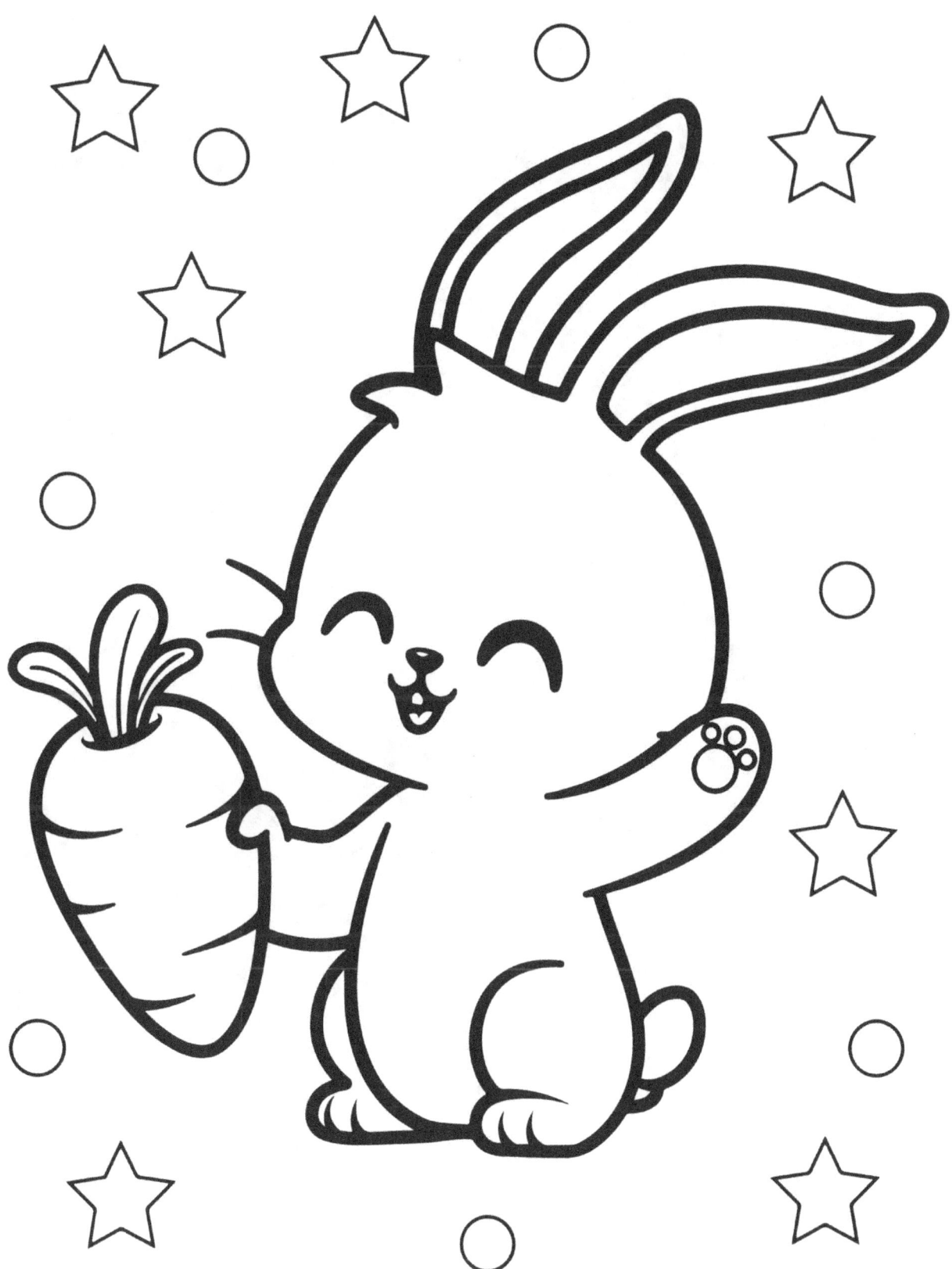

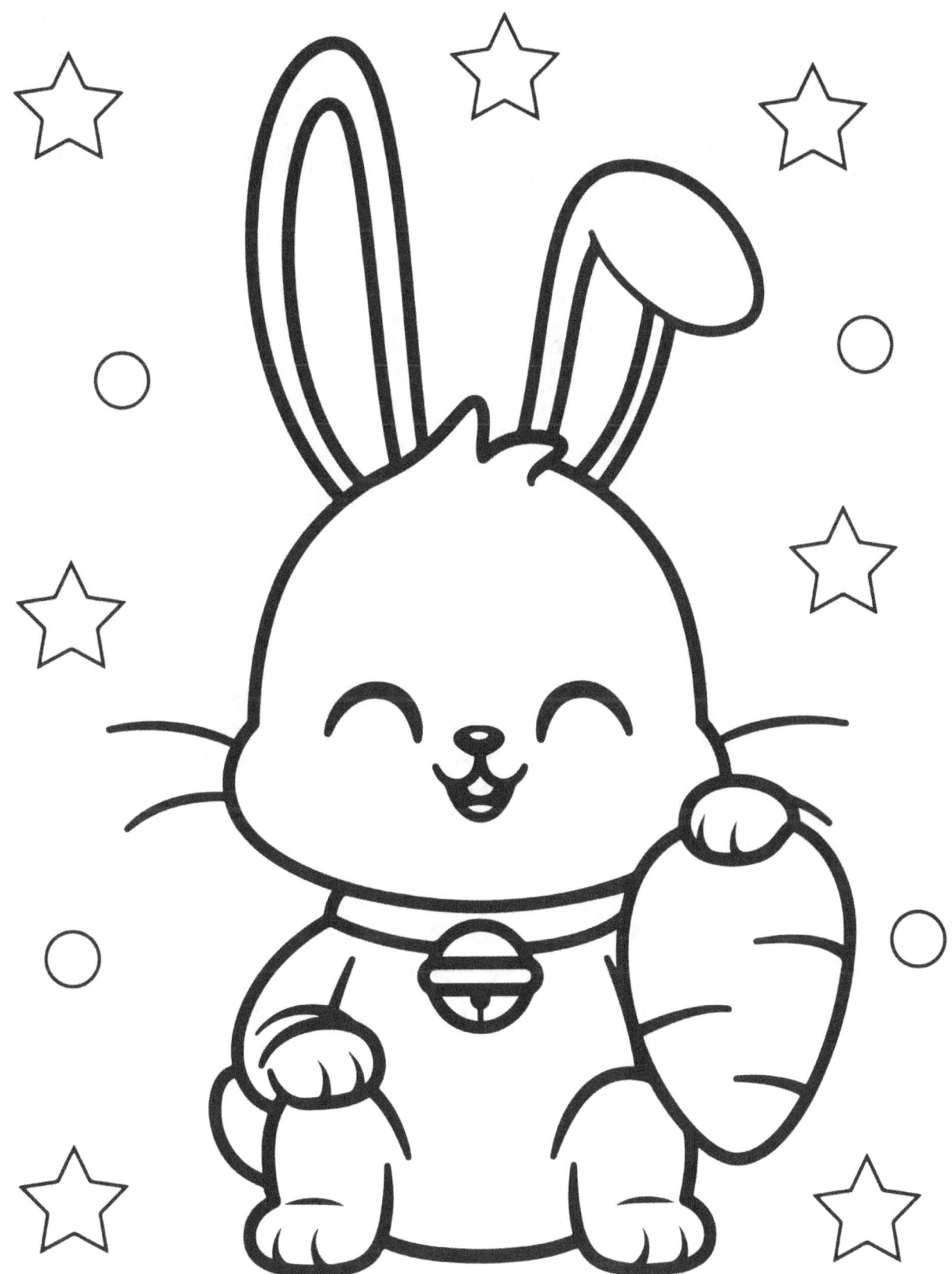

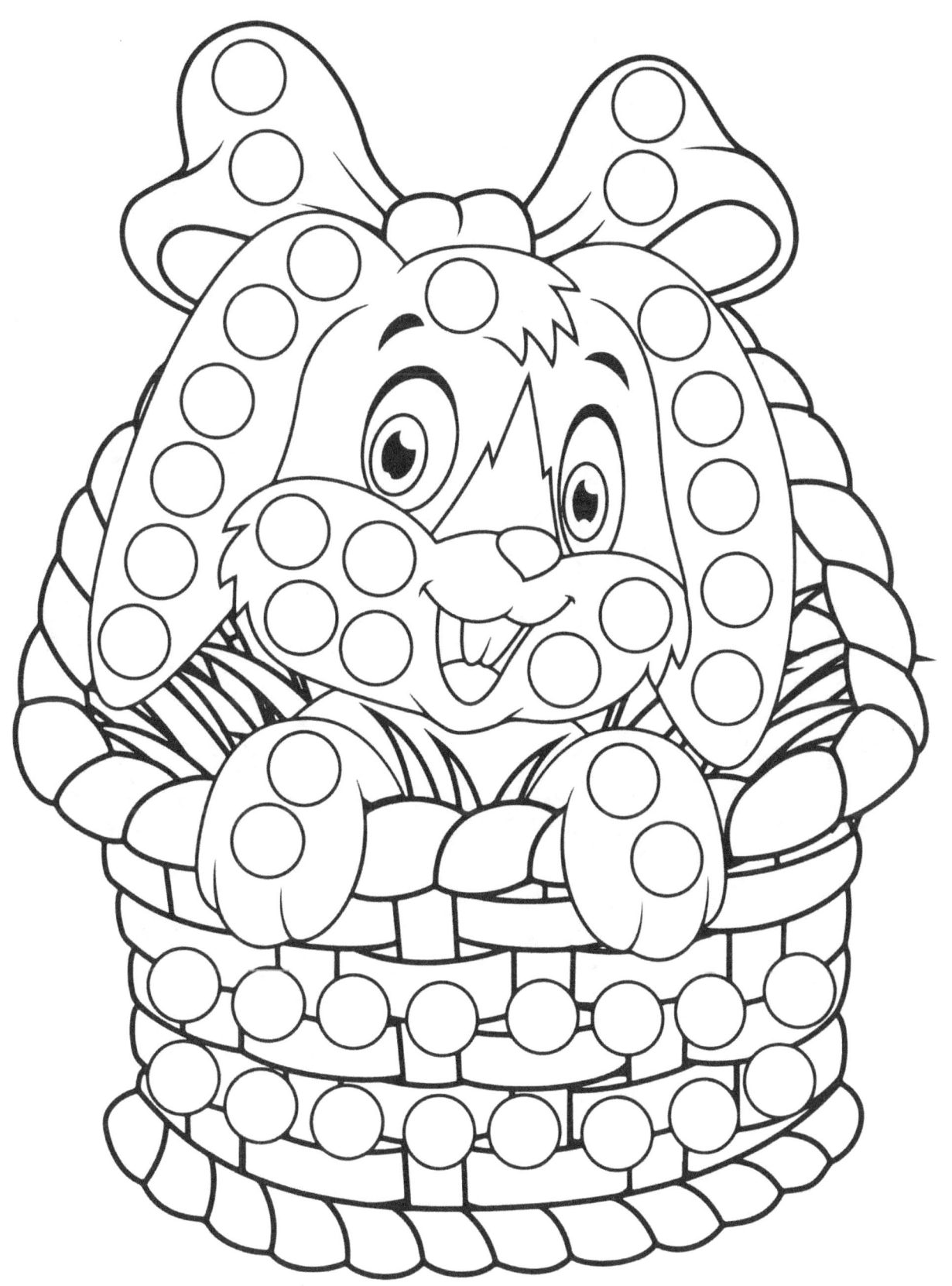

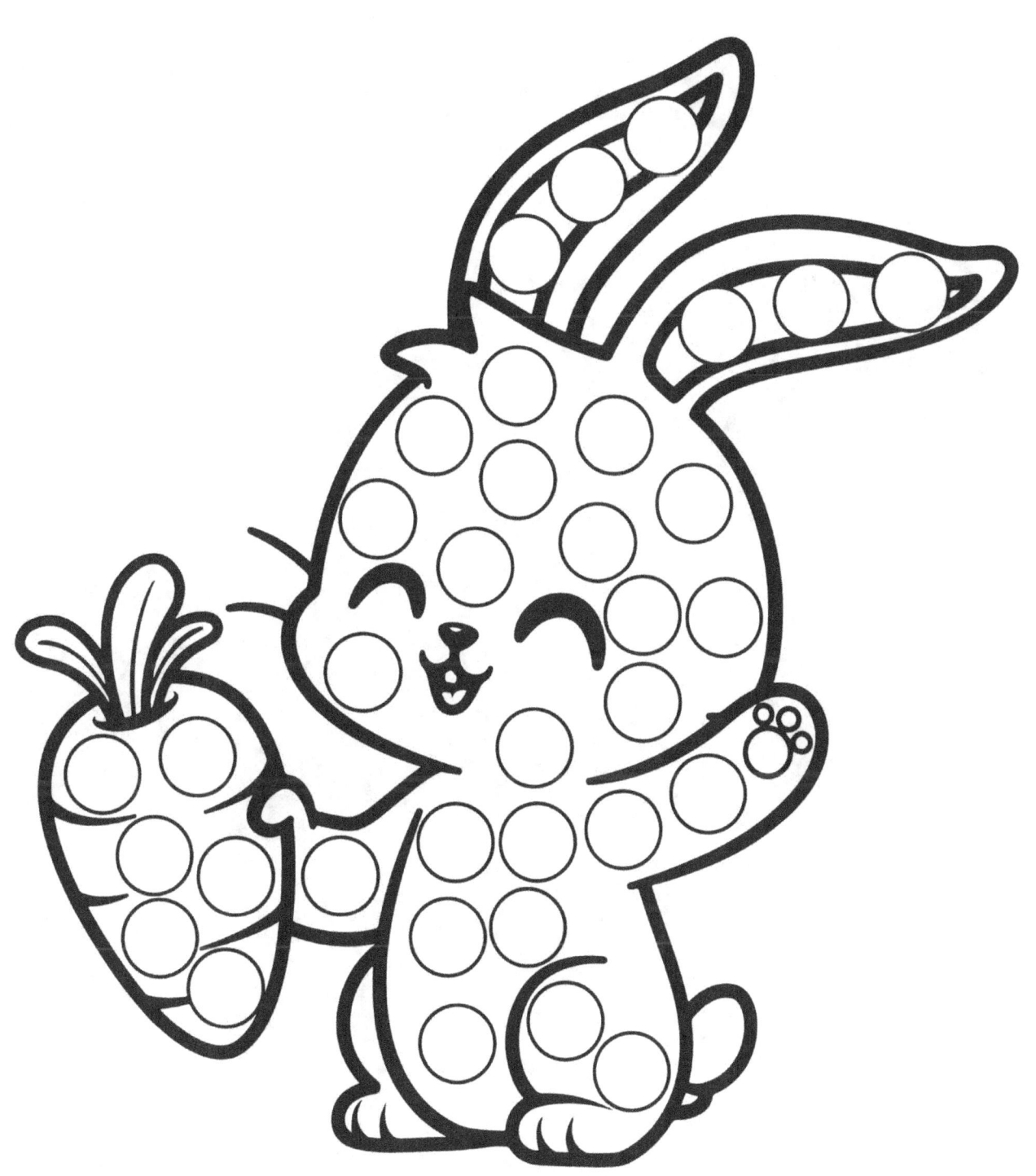

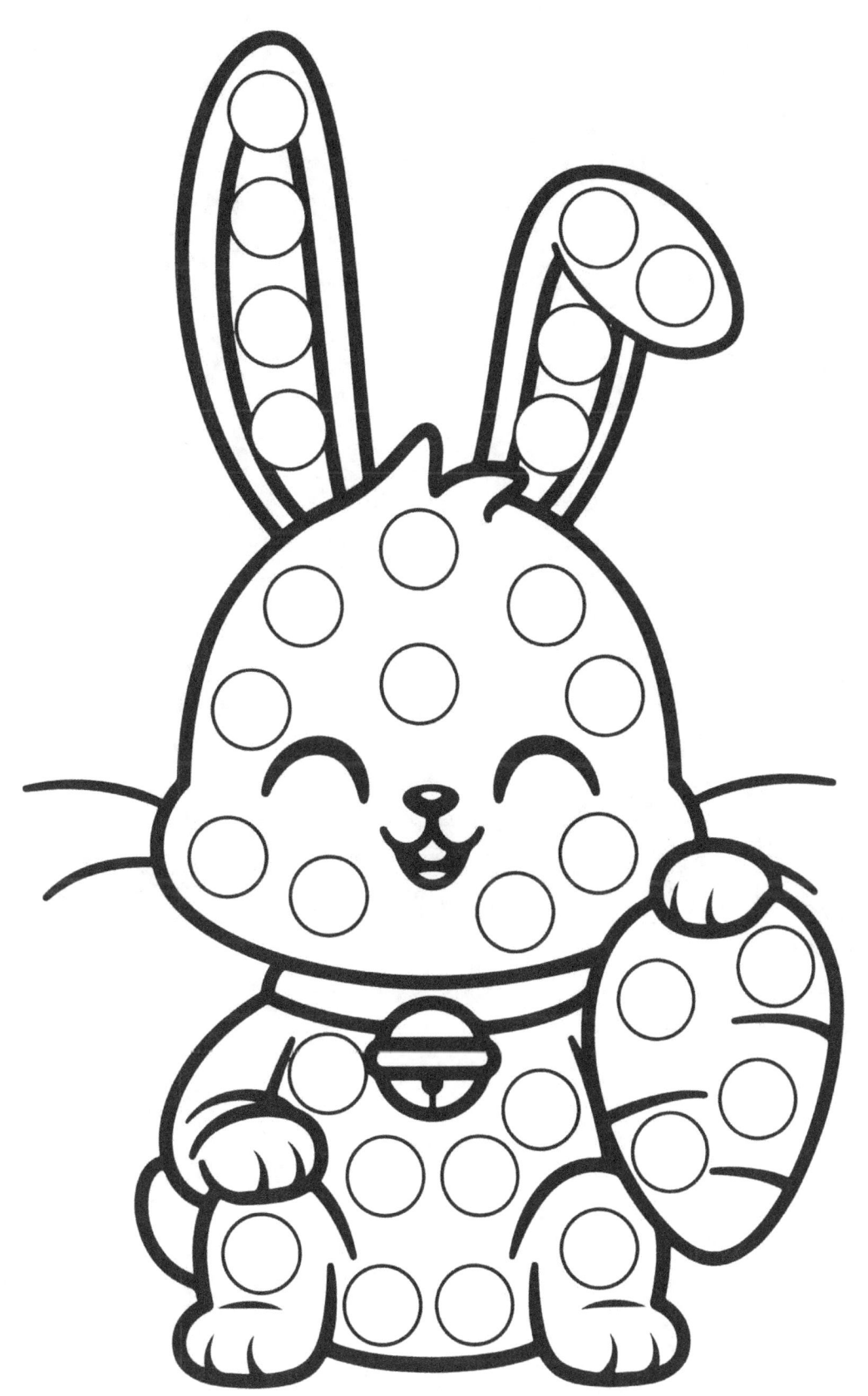

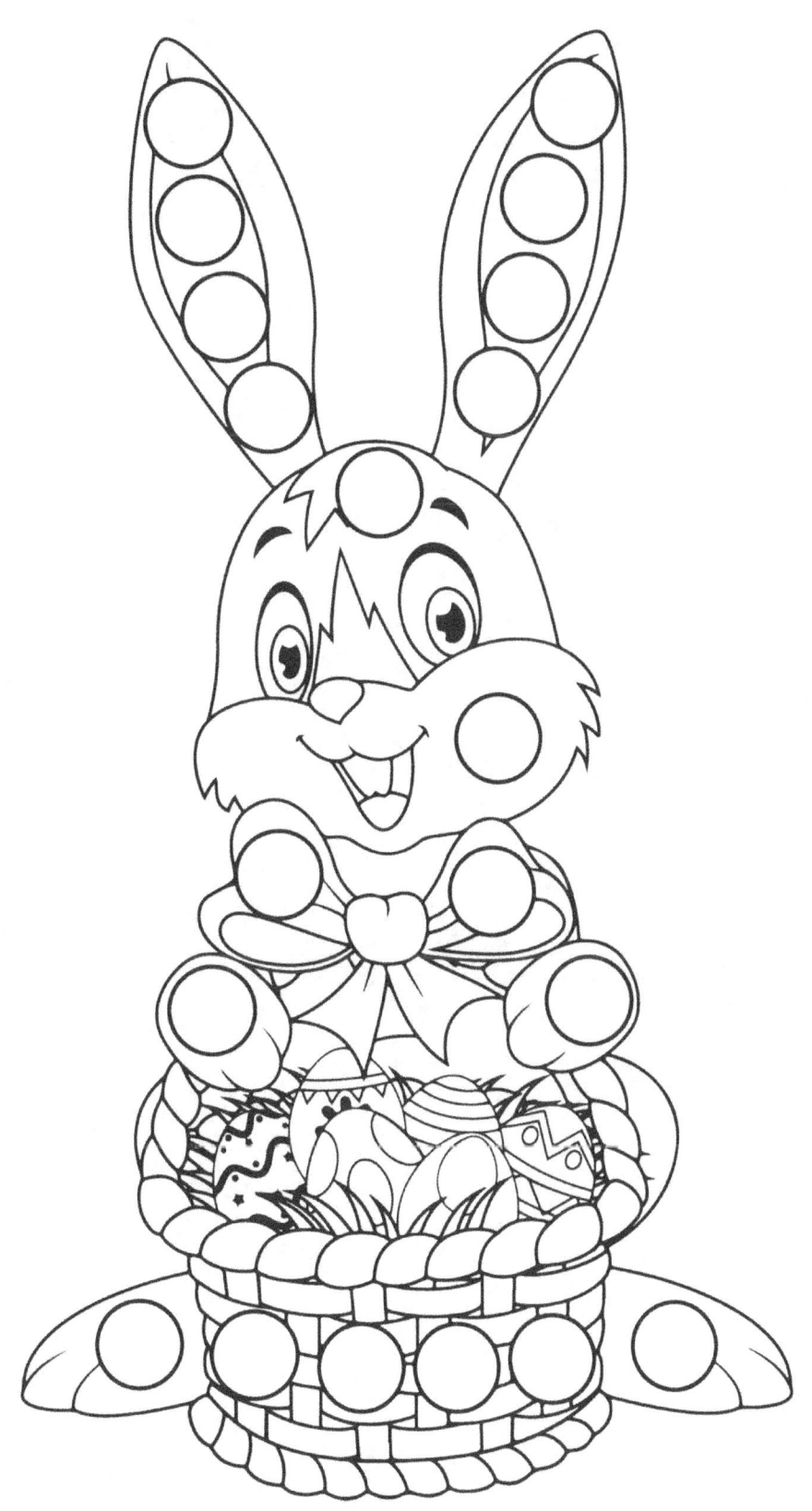

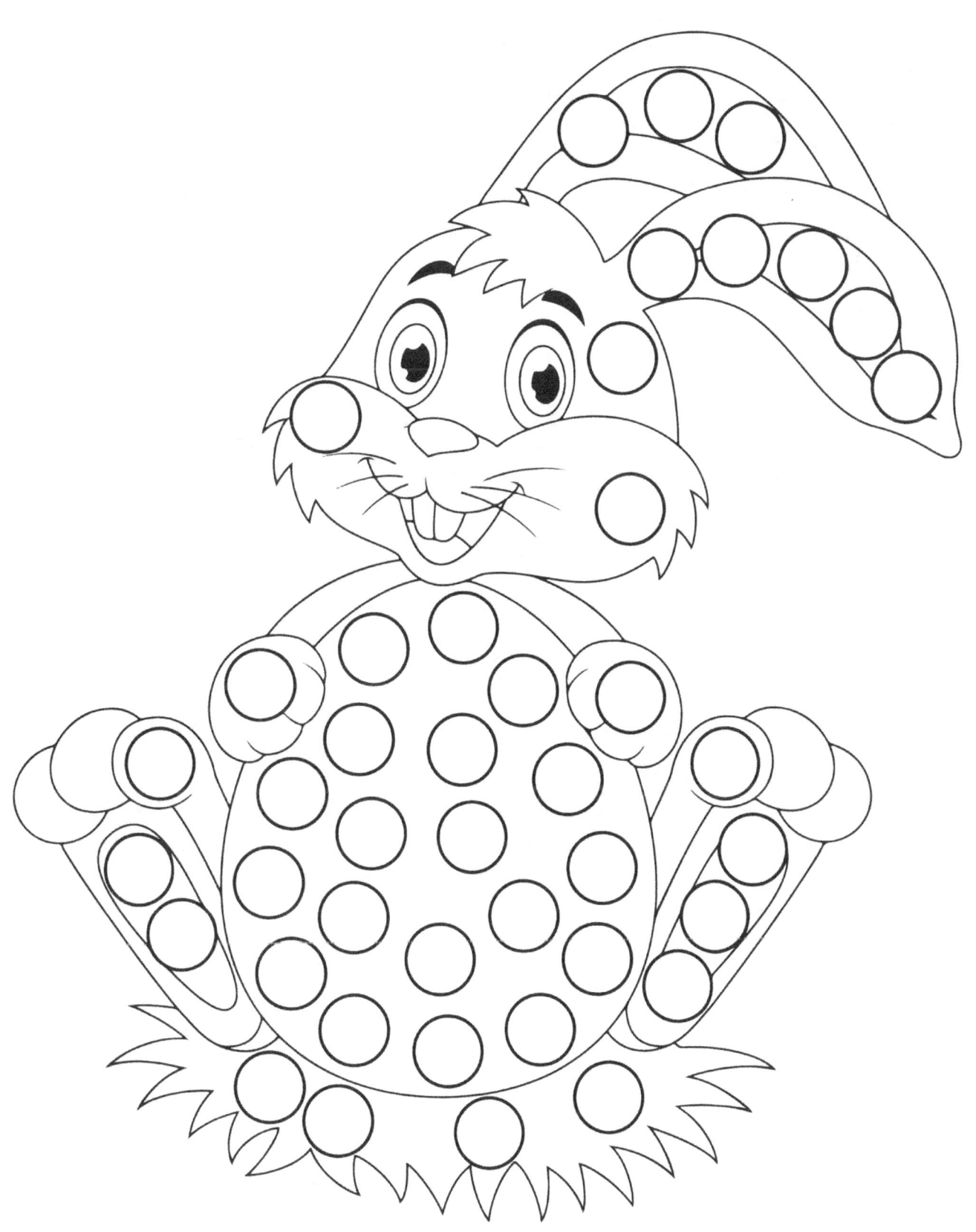

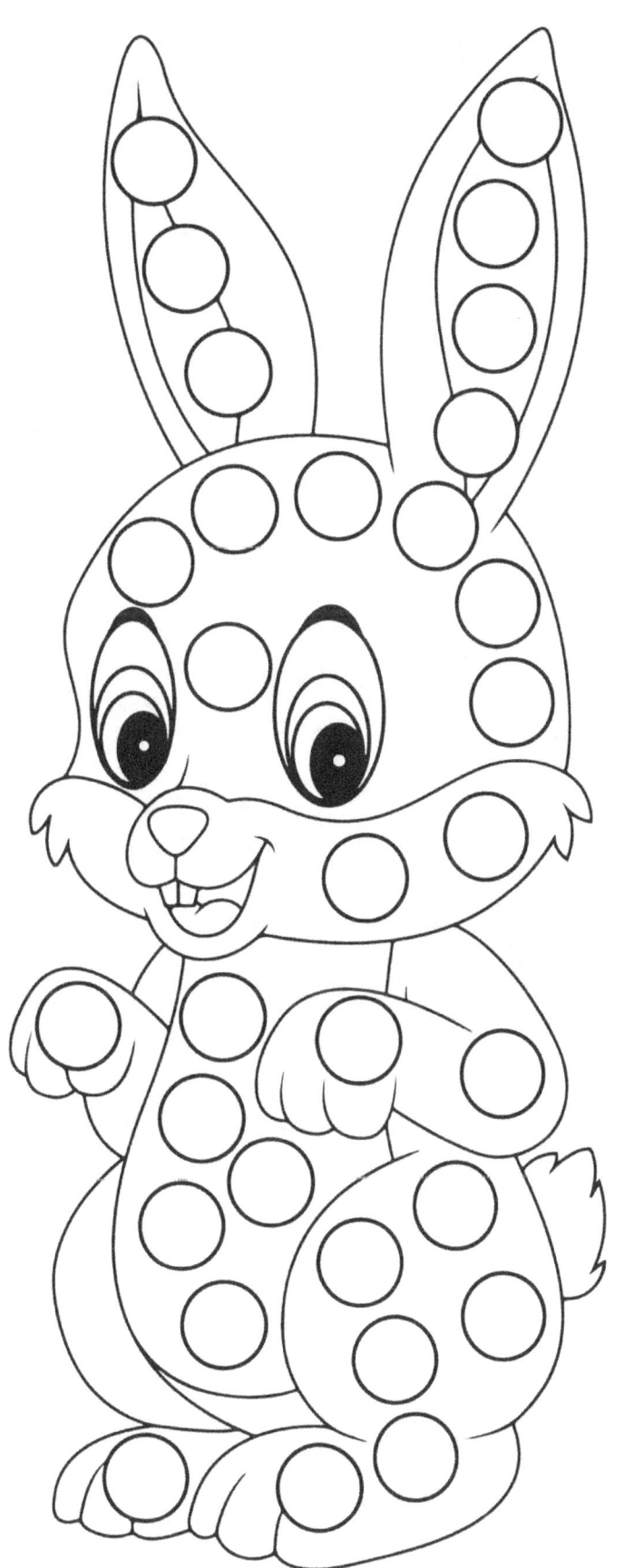

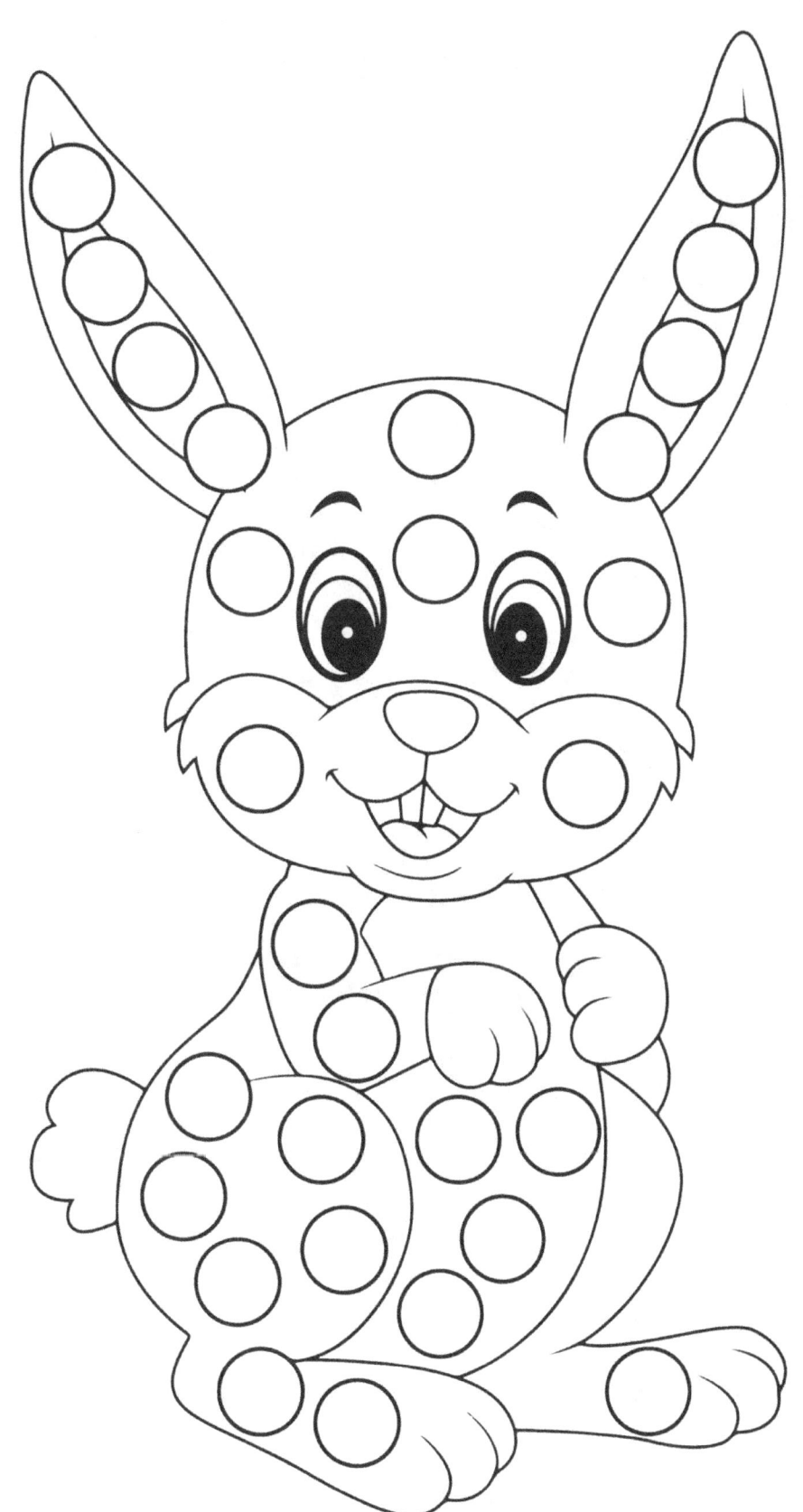

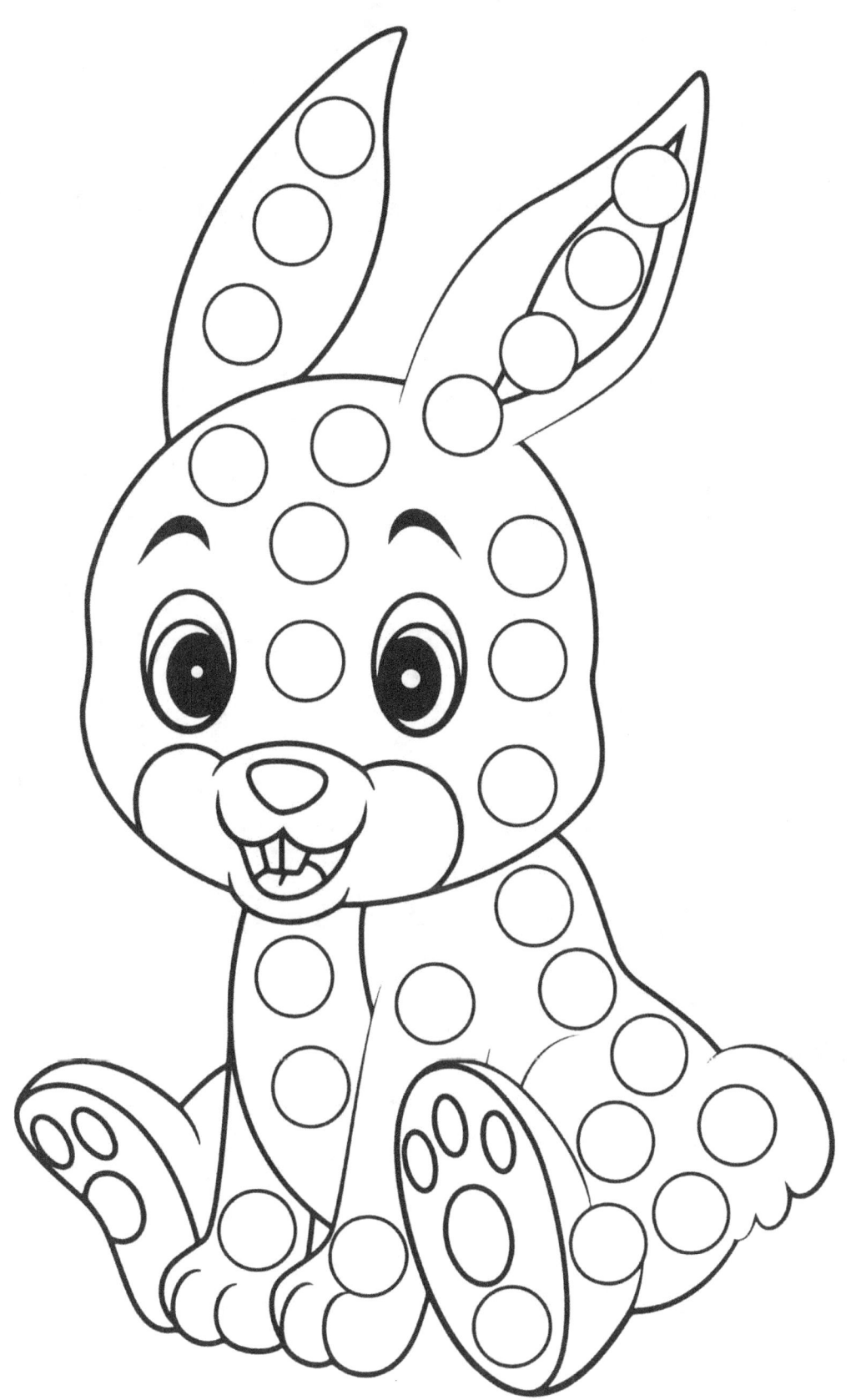

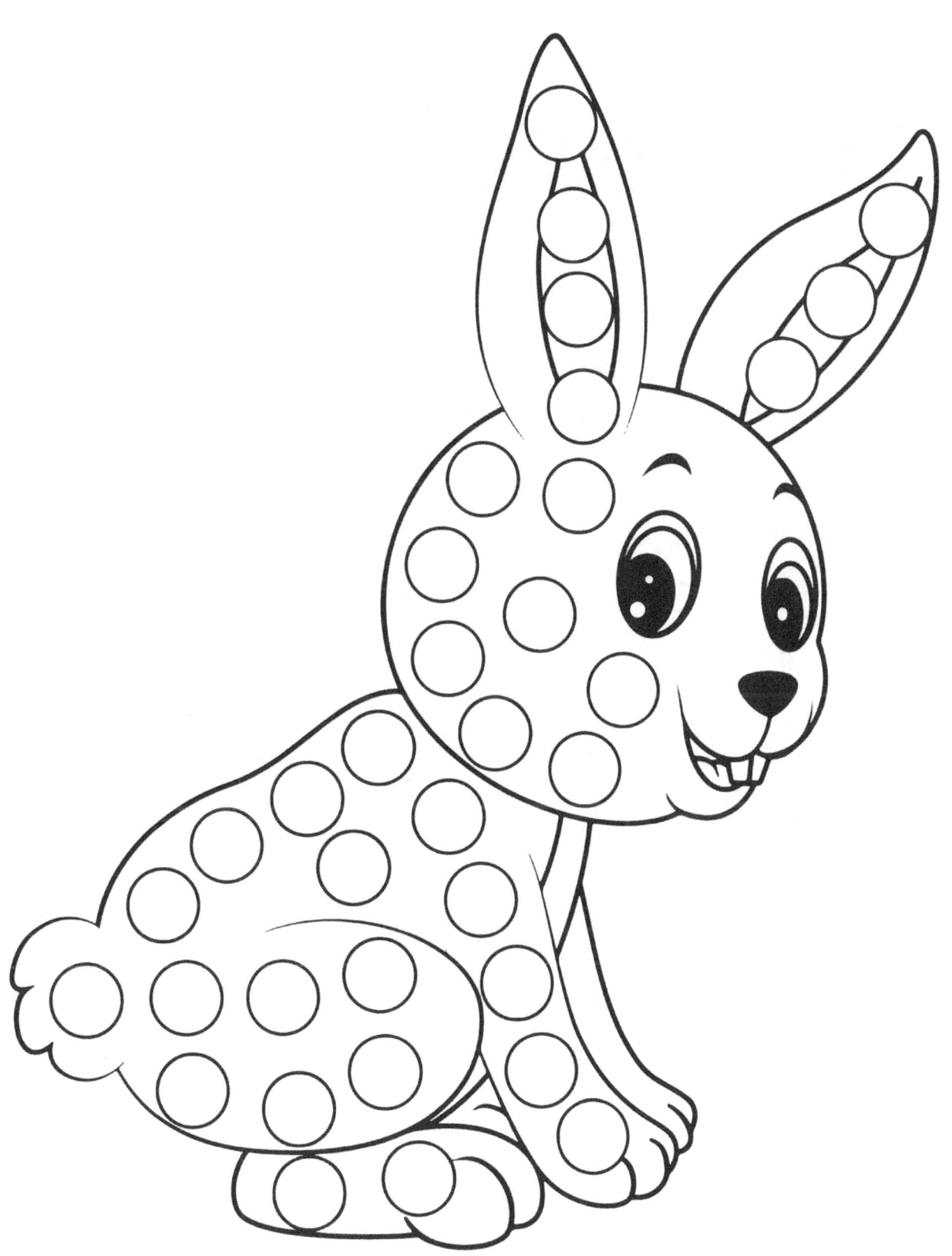

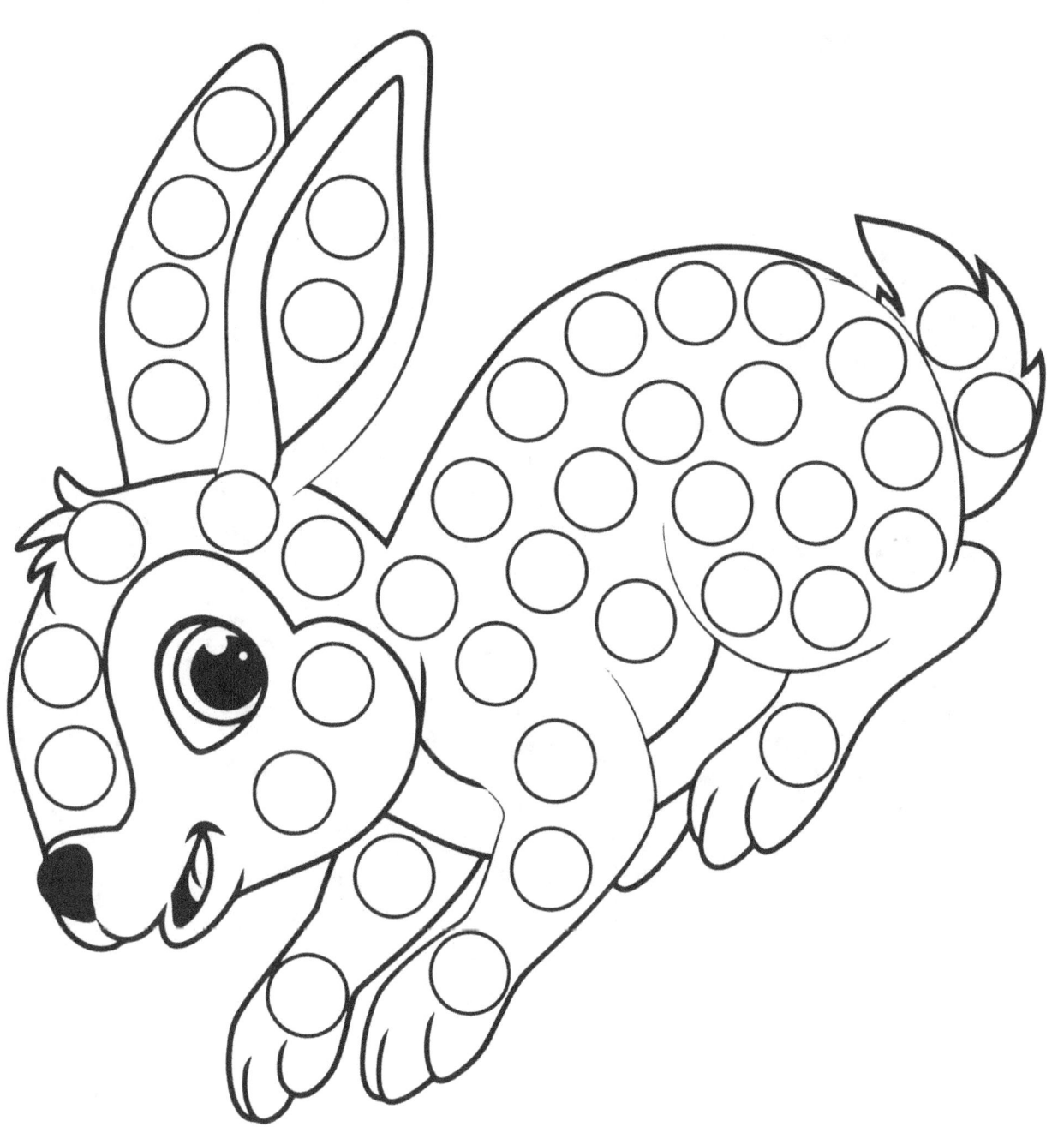

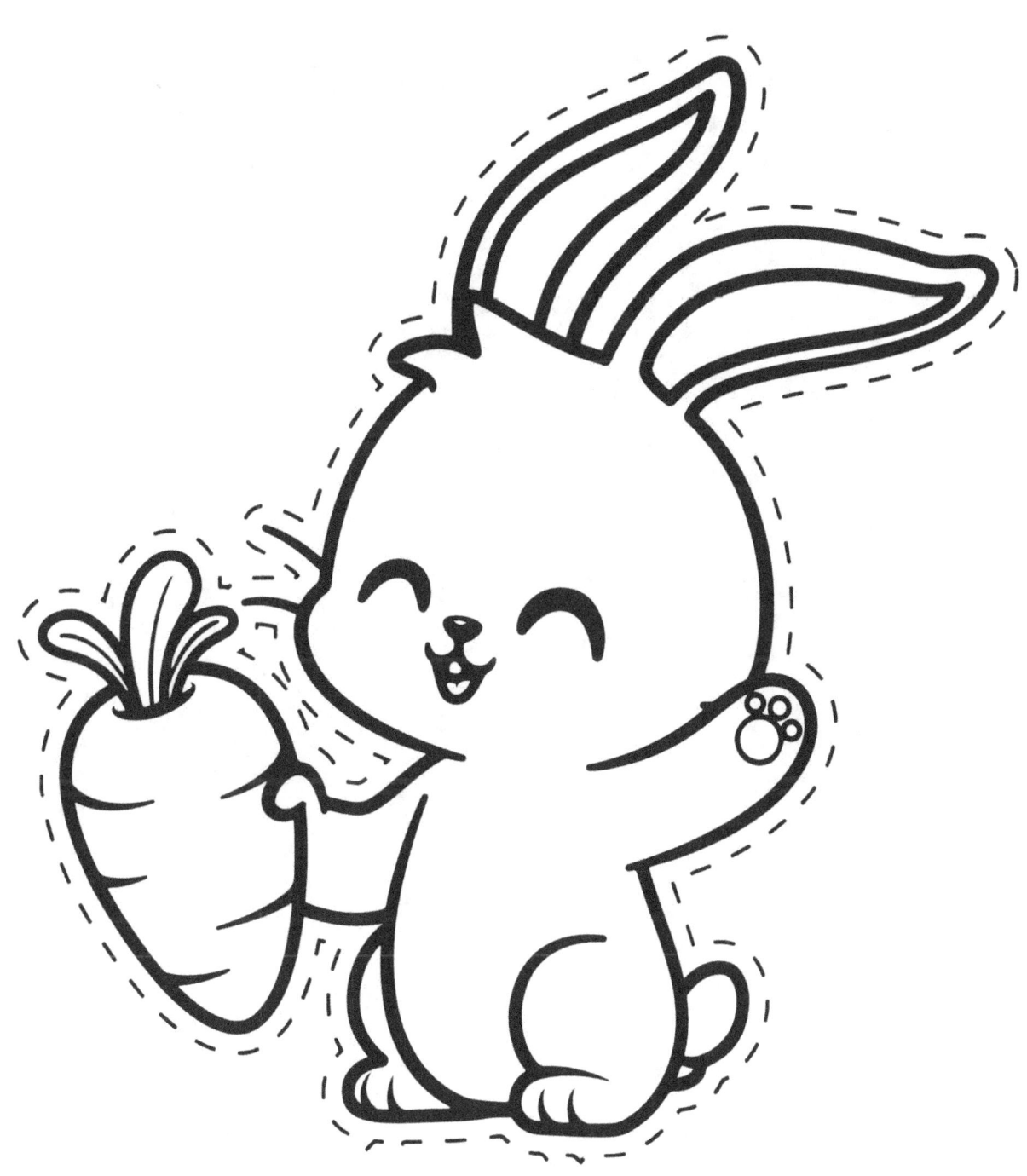

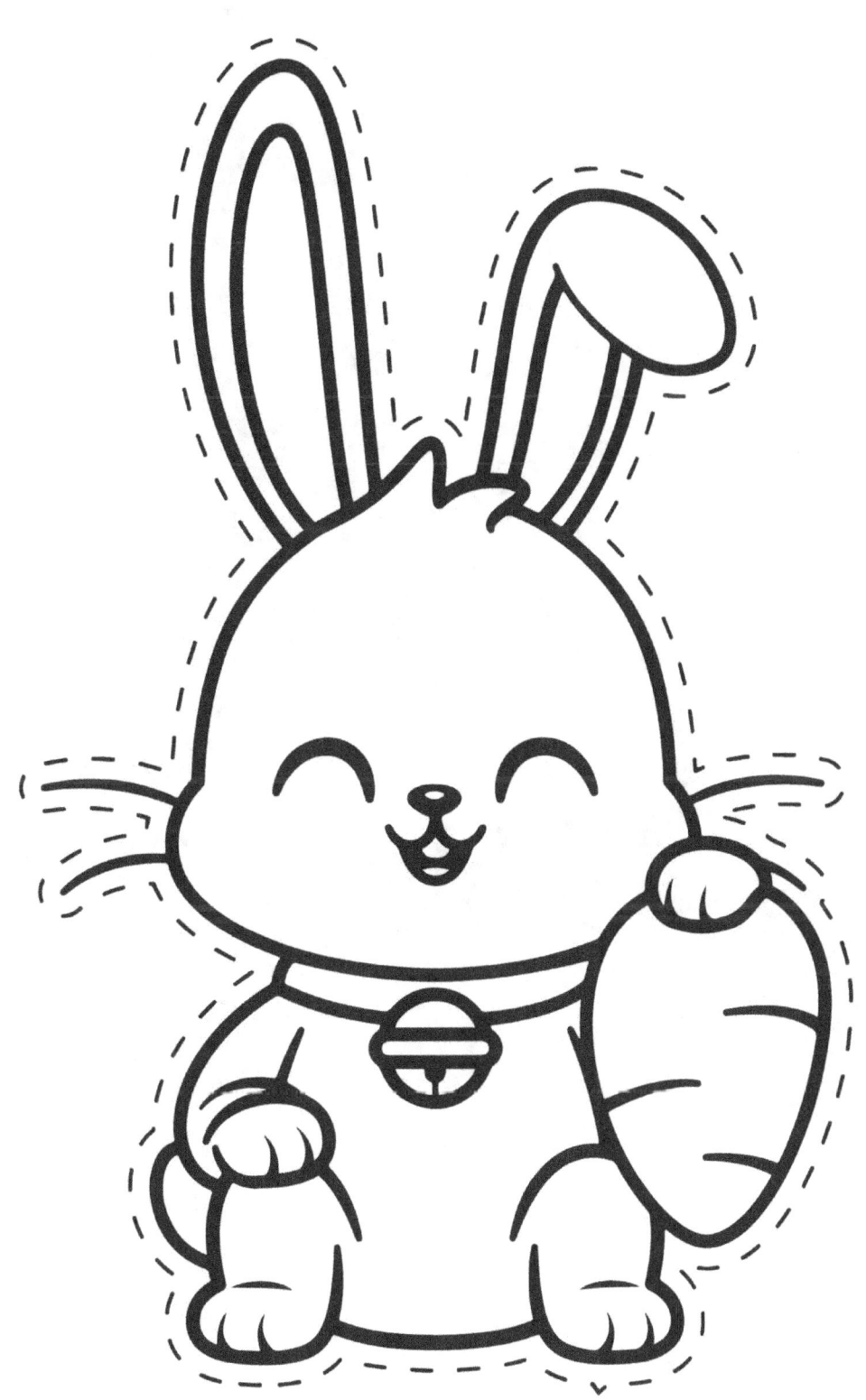

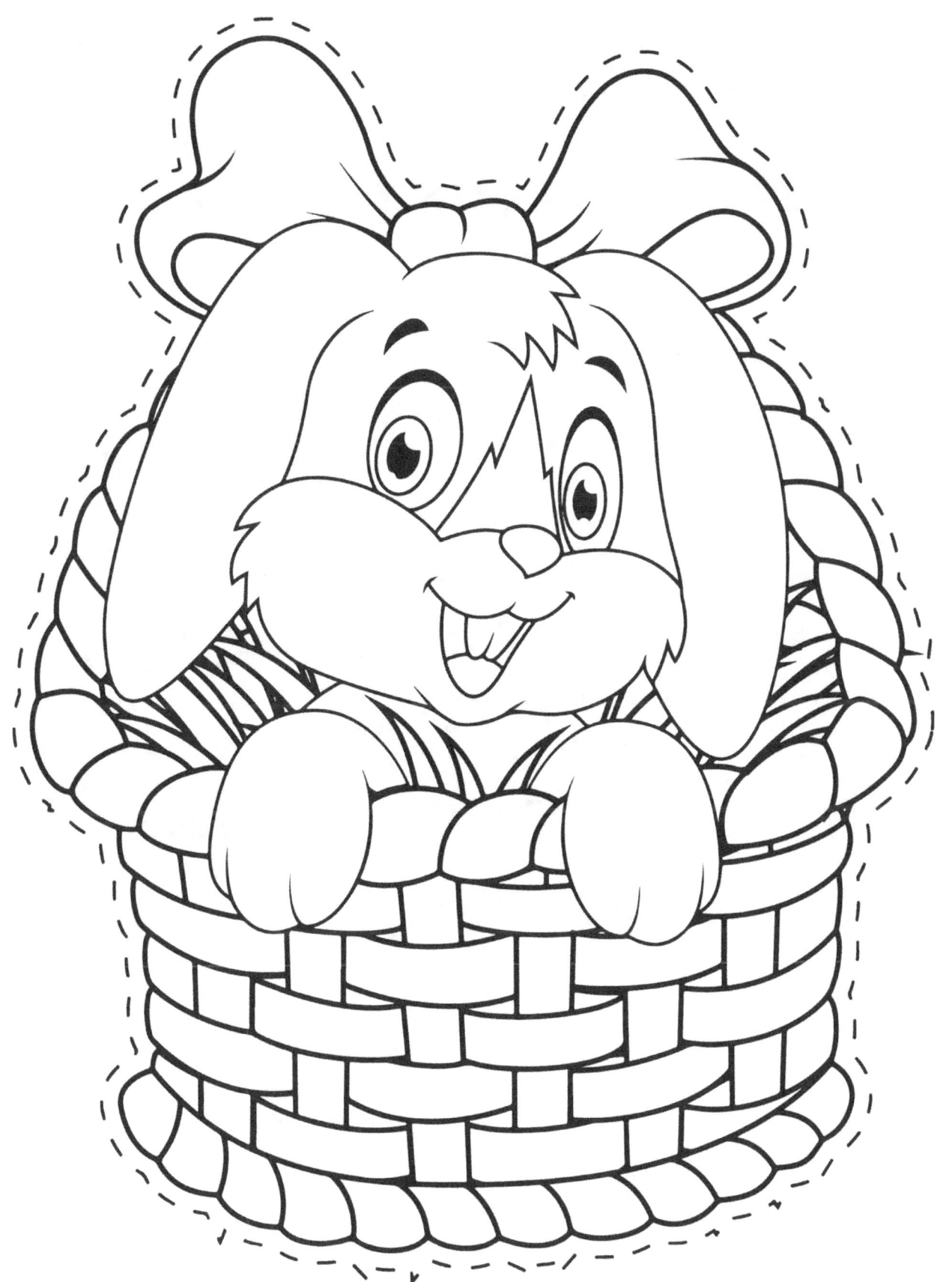

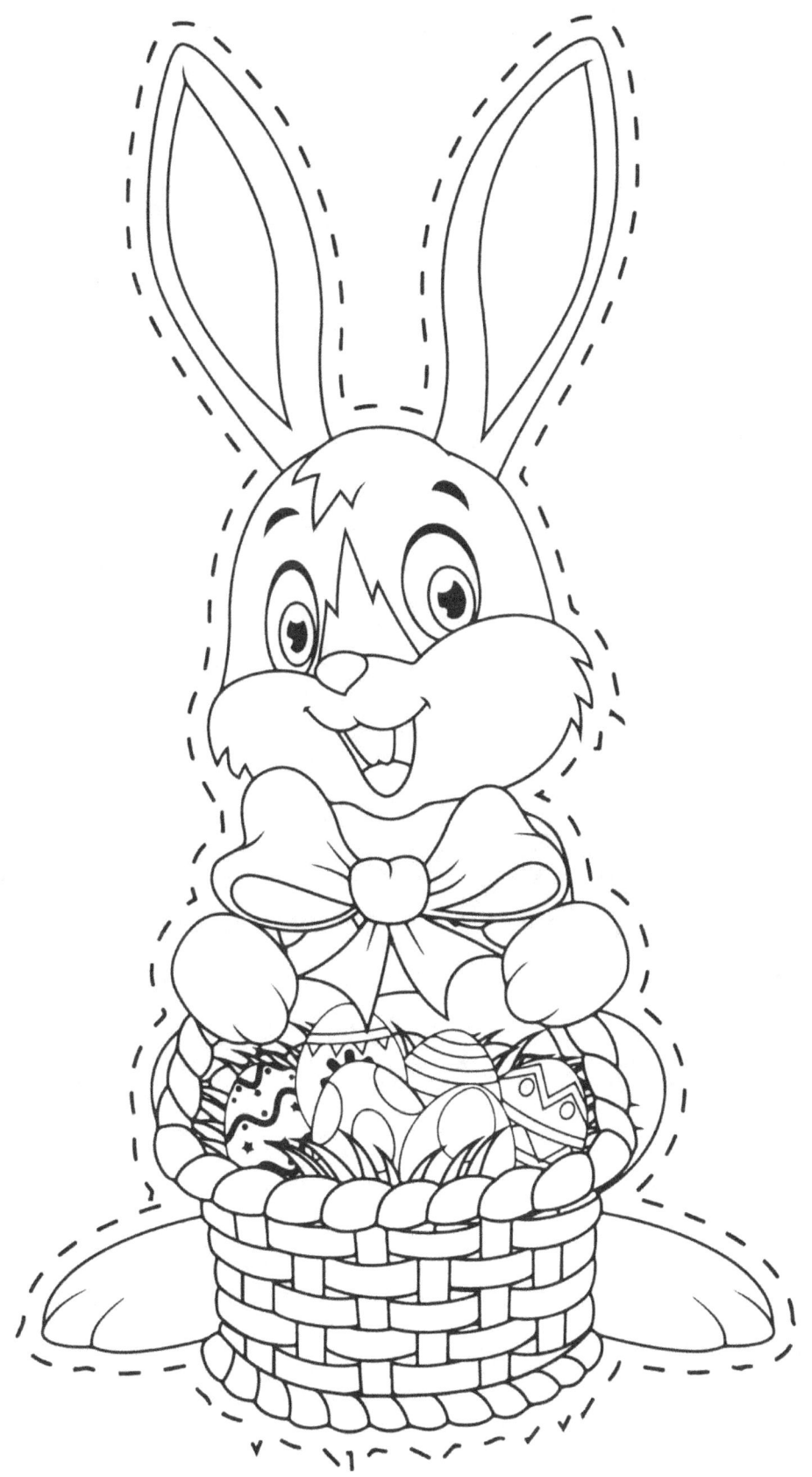

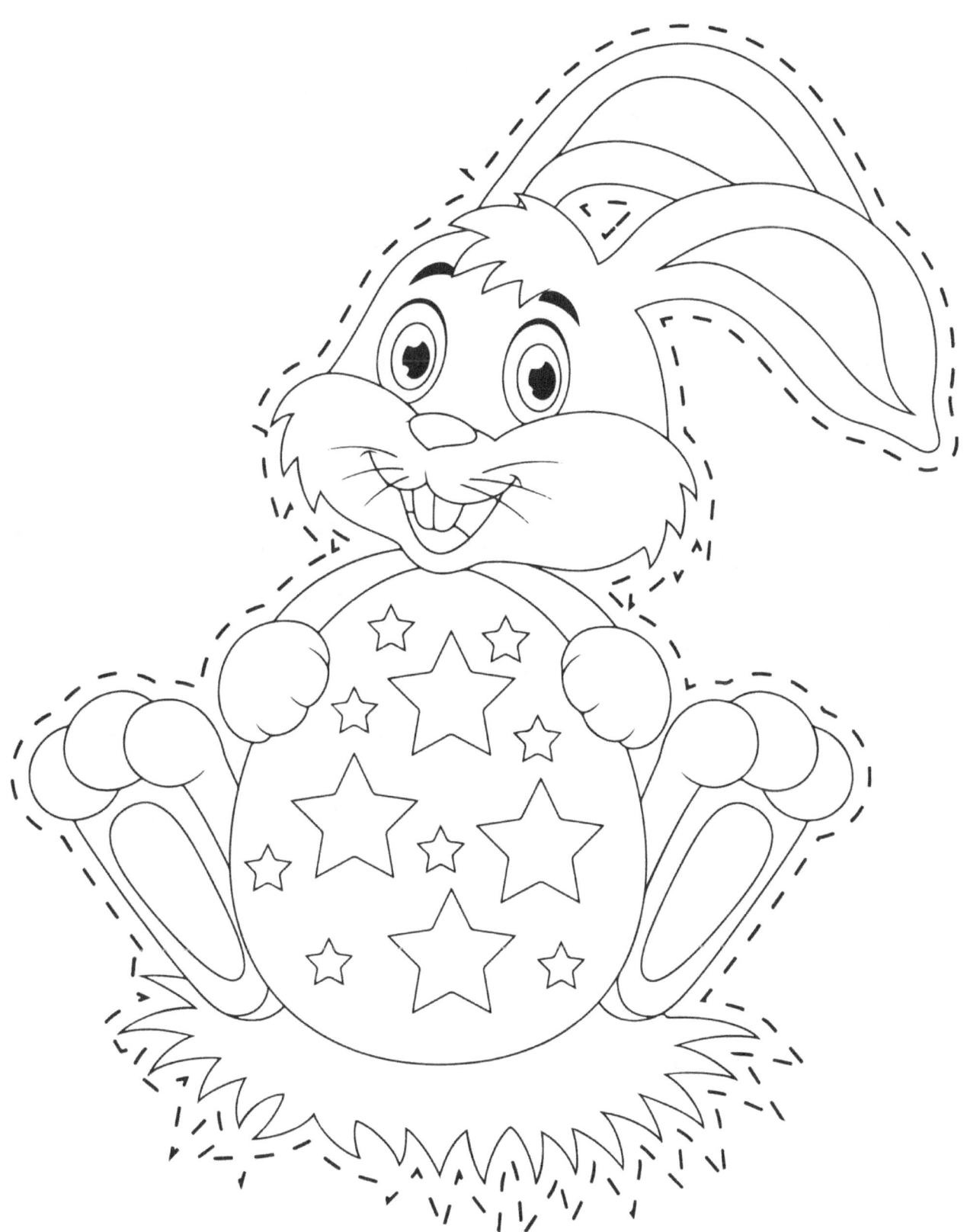

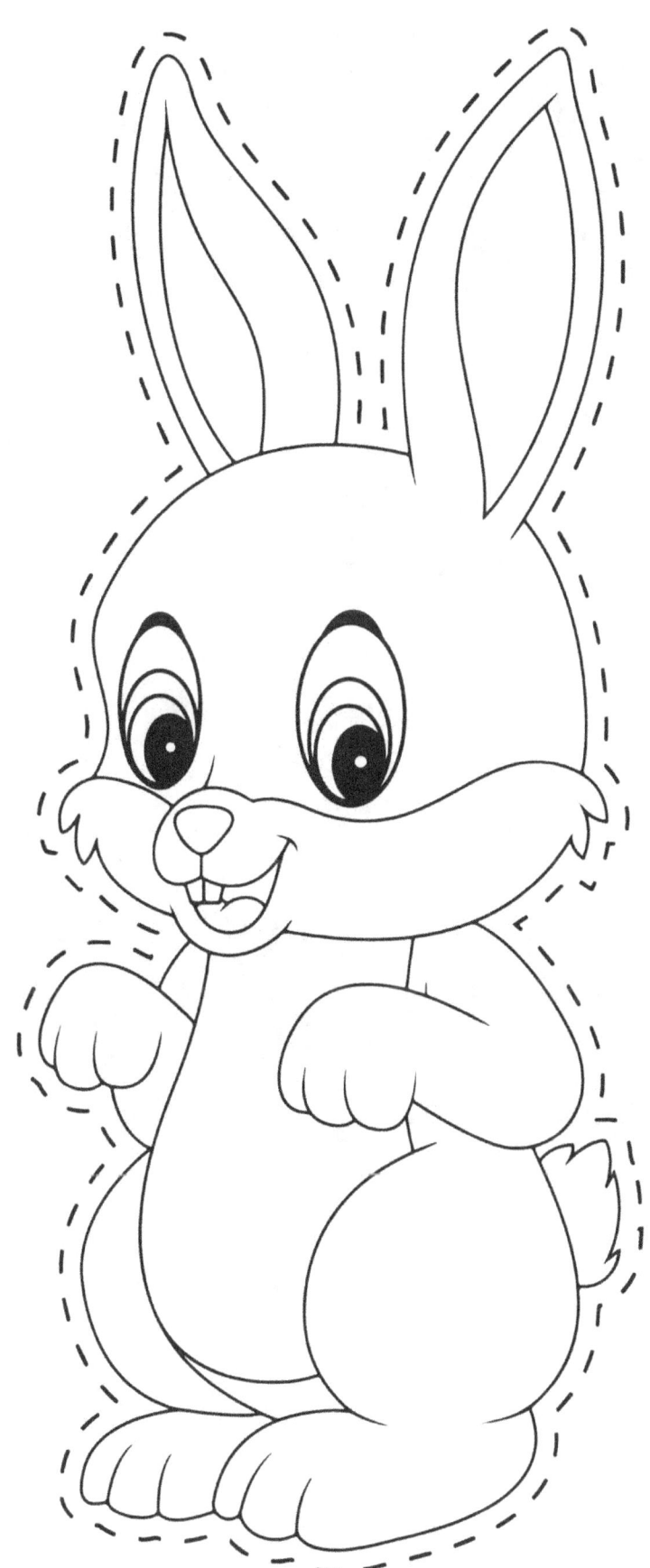

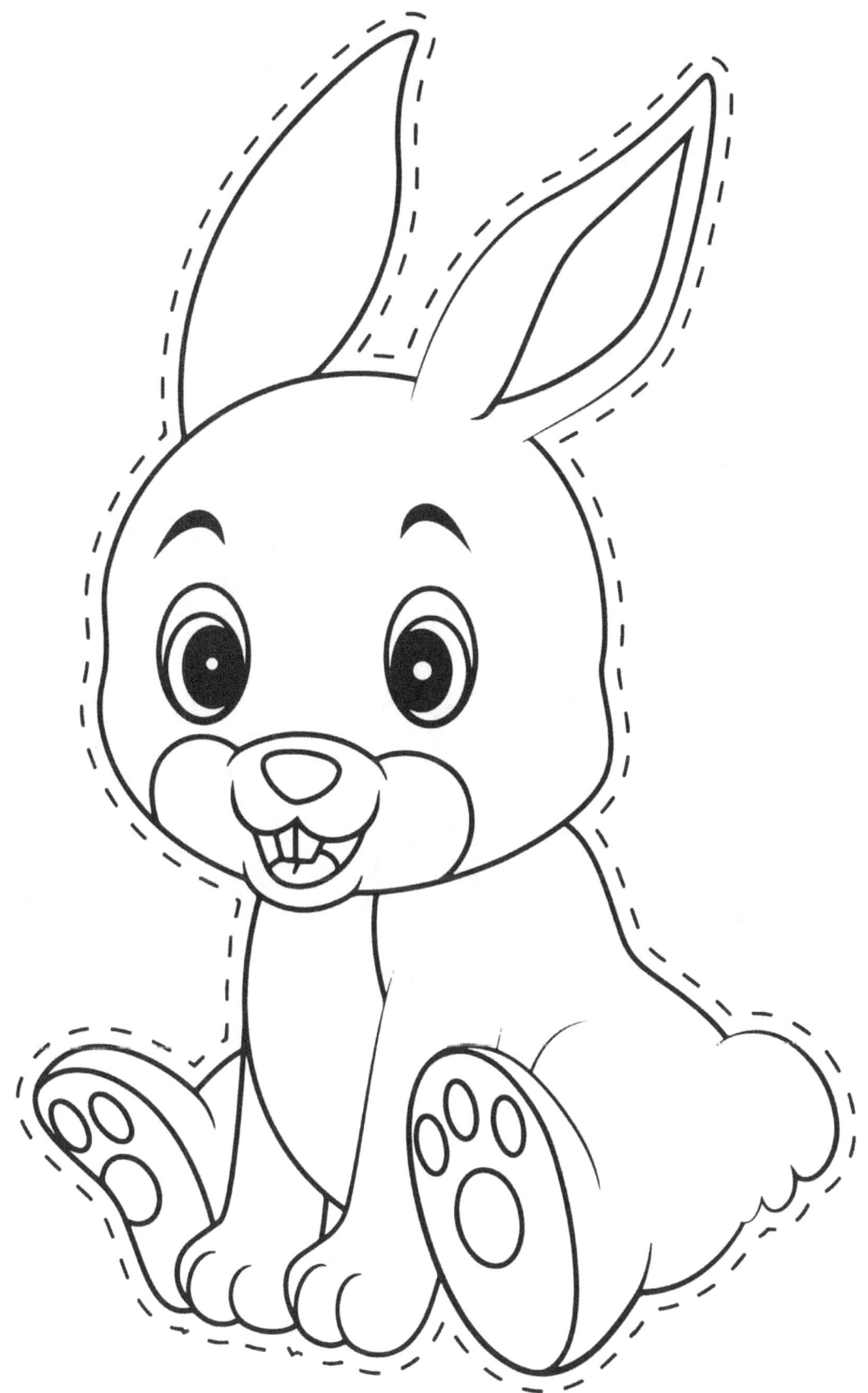

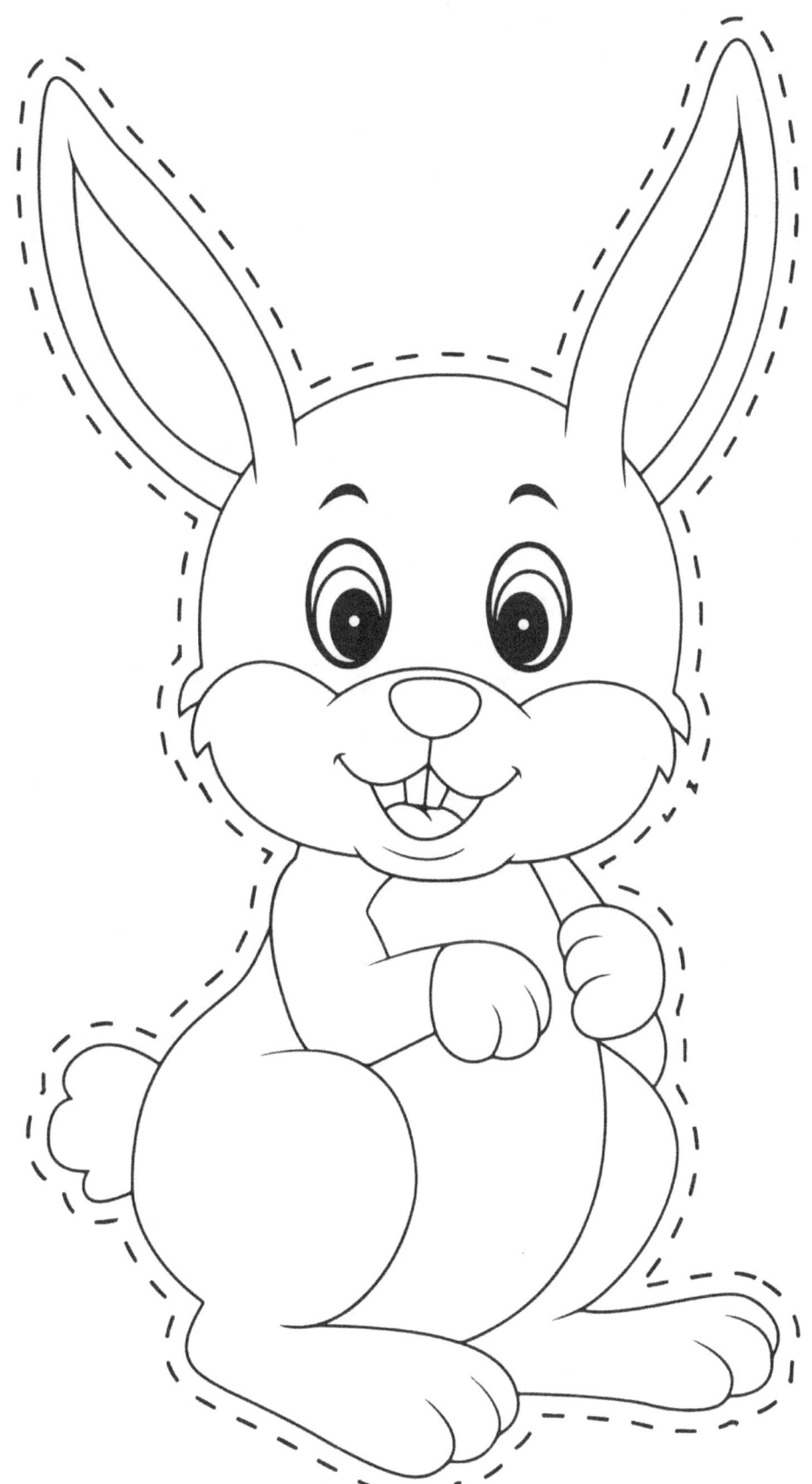

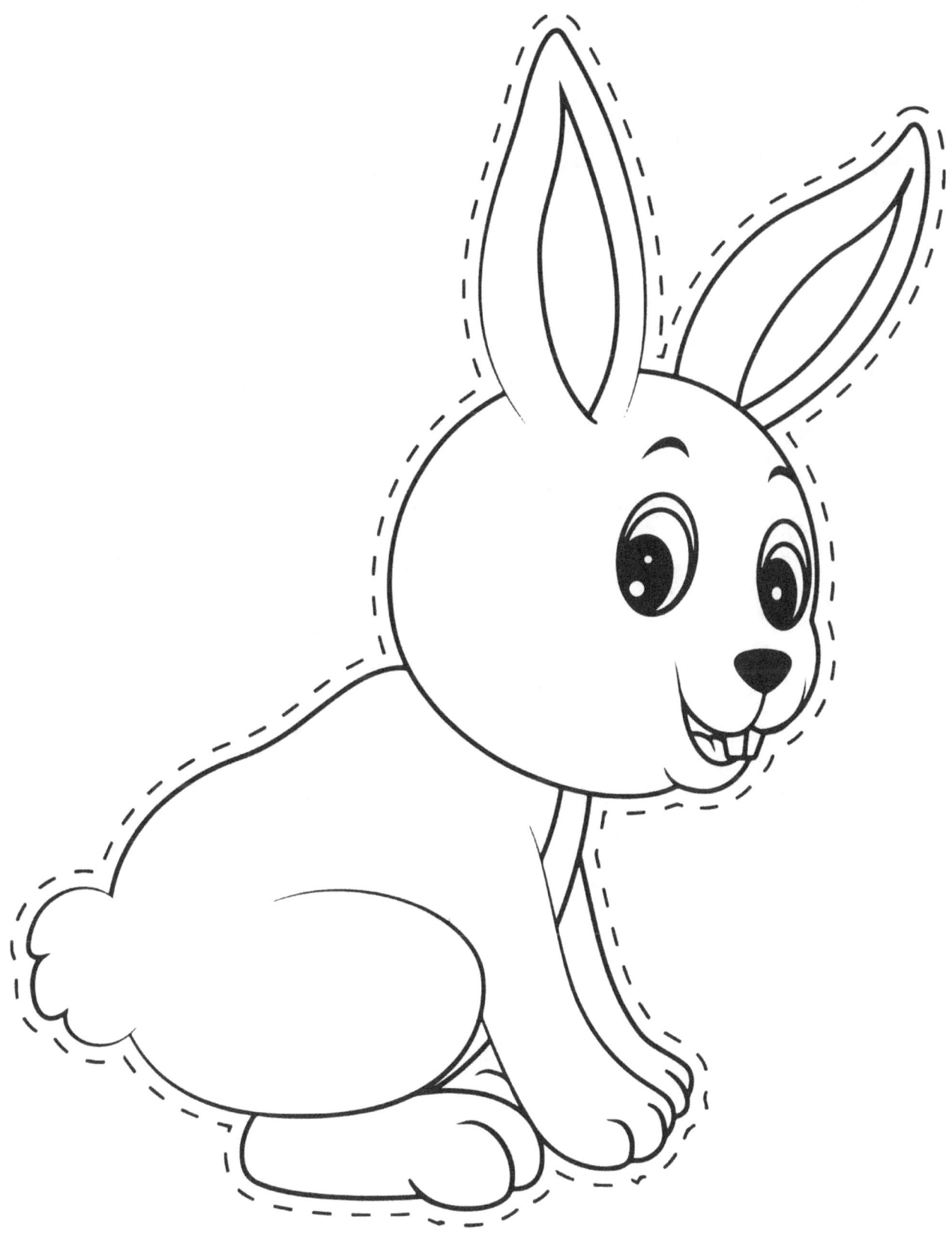

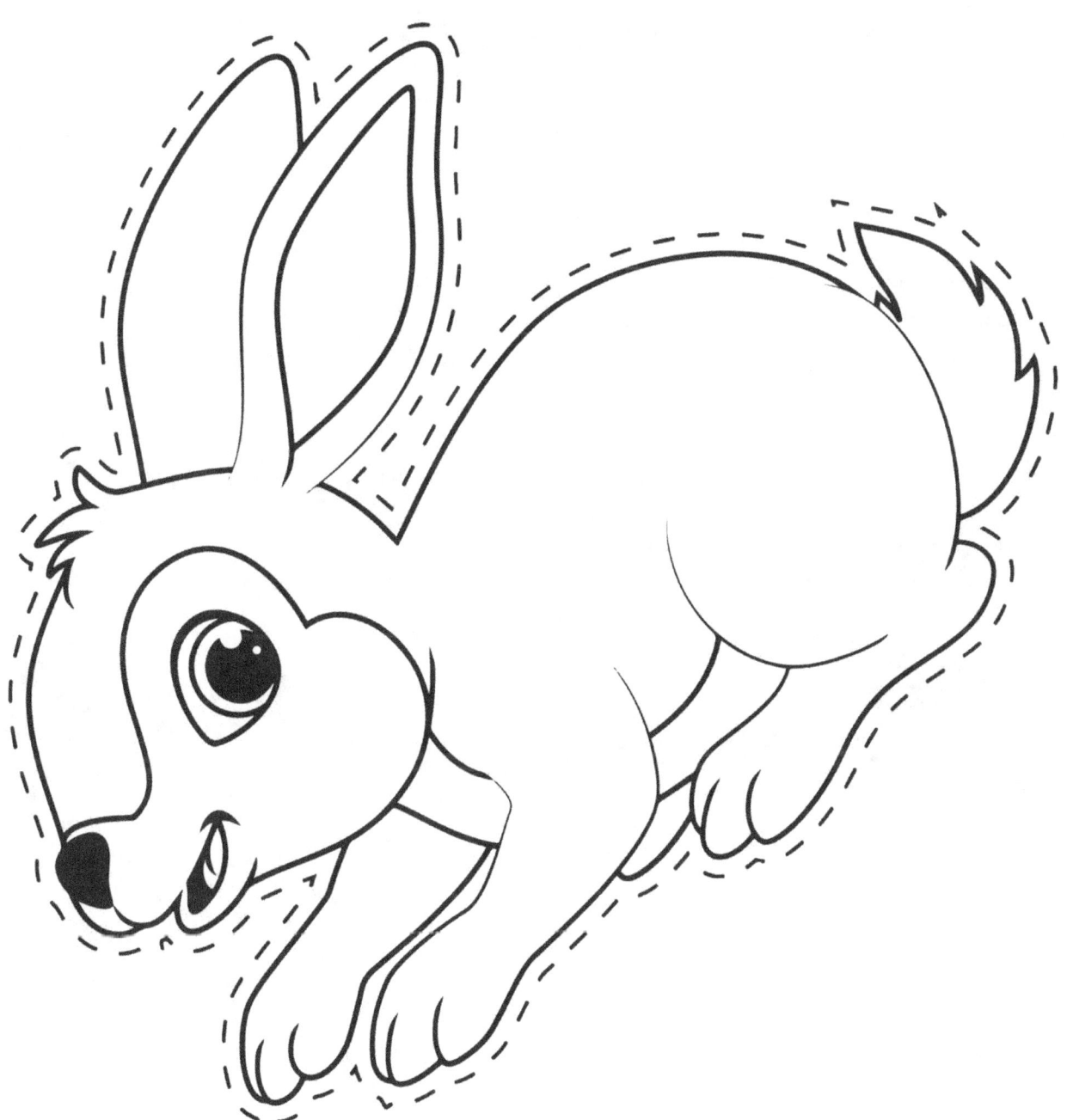

Name:..........................

+ Connect The Dots With Numbers
+ Color The Picture Brightly

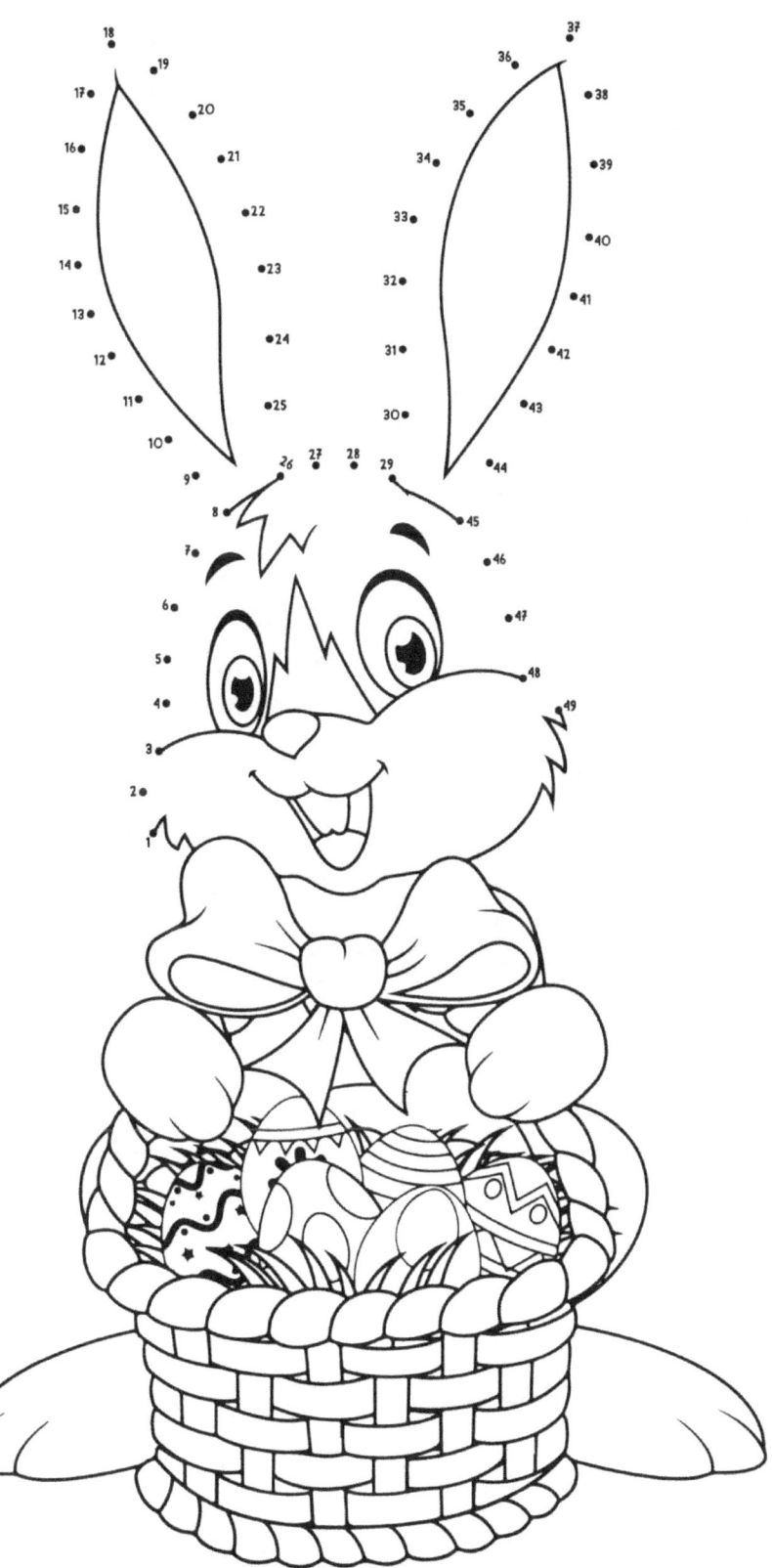

Name:......................... + Connect The Dots With Numbers
+ Color The Picture Brightly

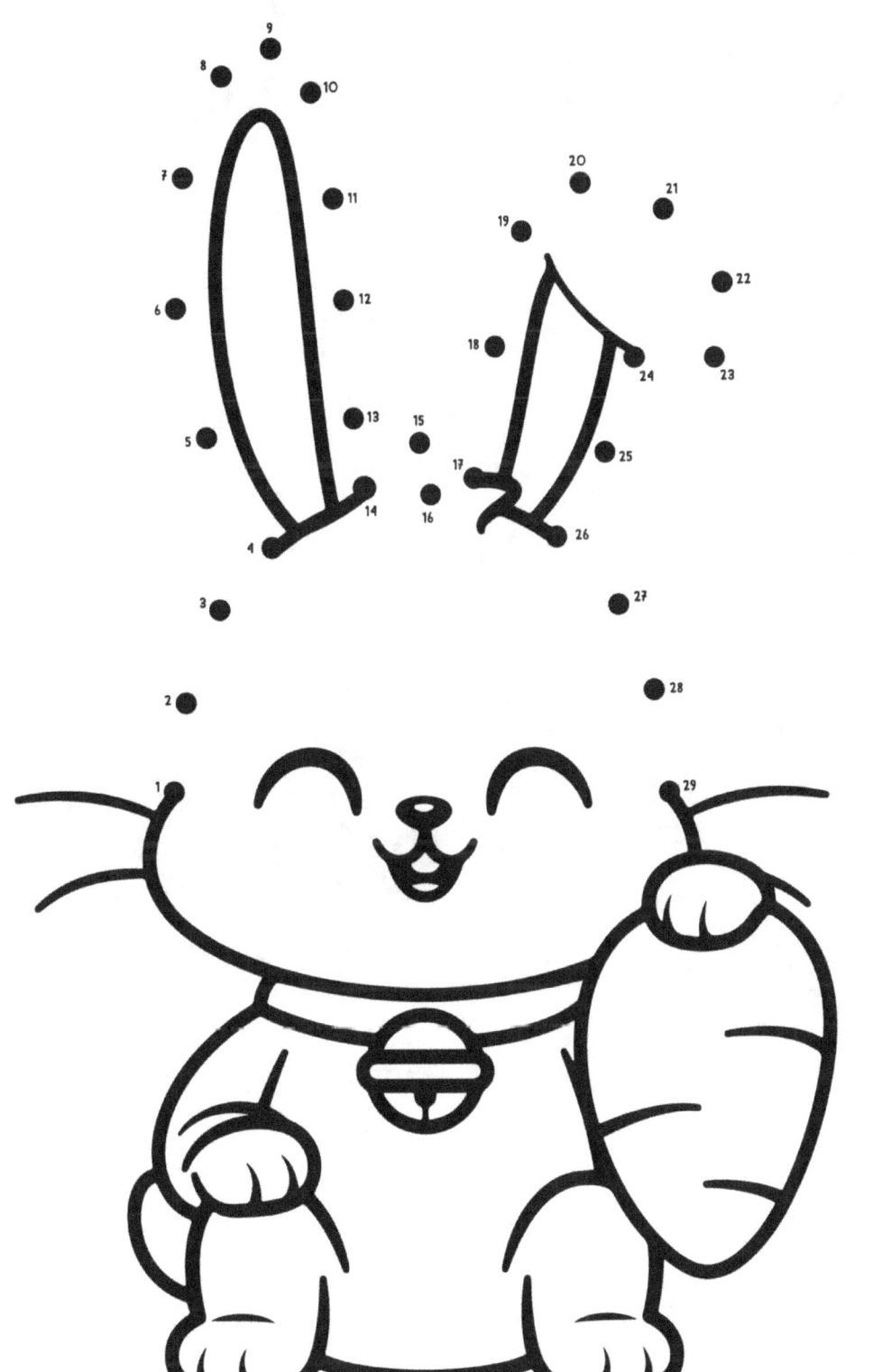

Name:........................

+ Connect The Dots With Numbers
+ Color The Picture Brightly

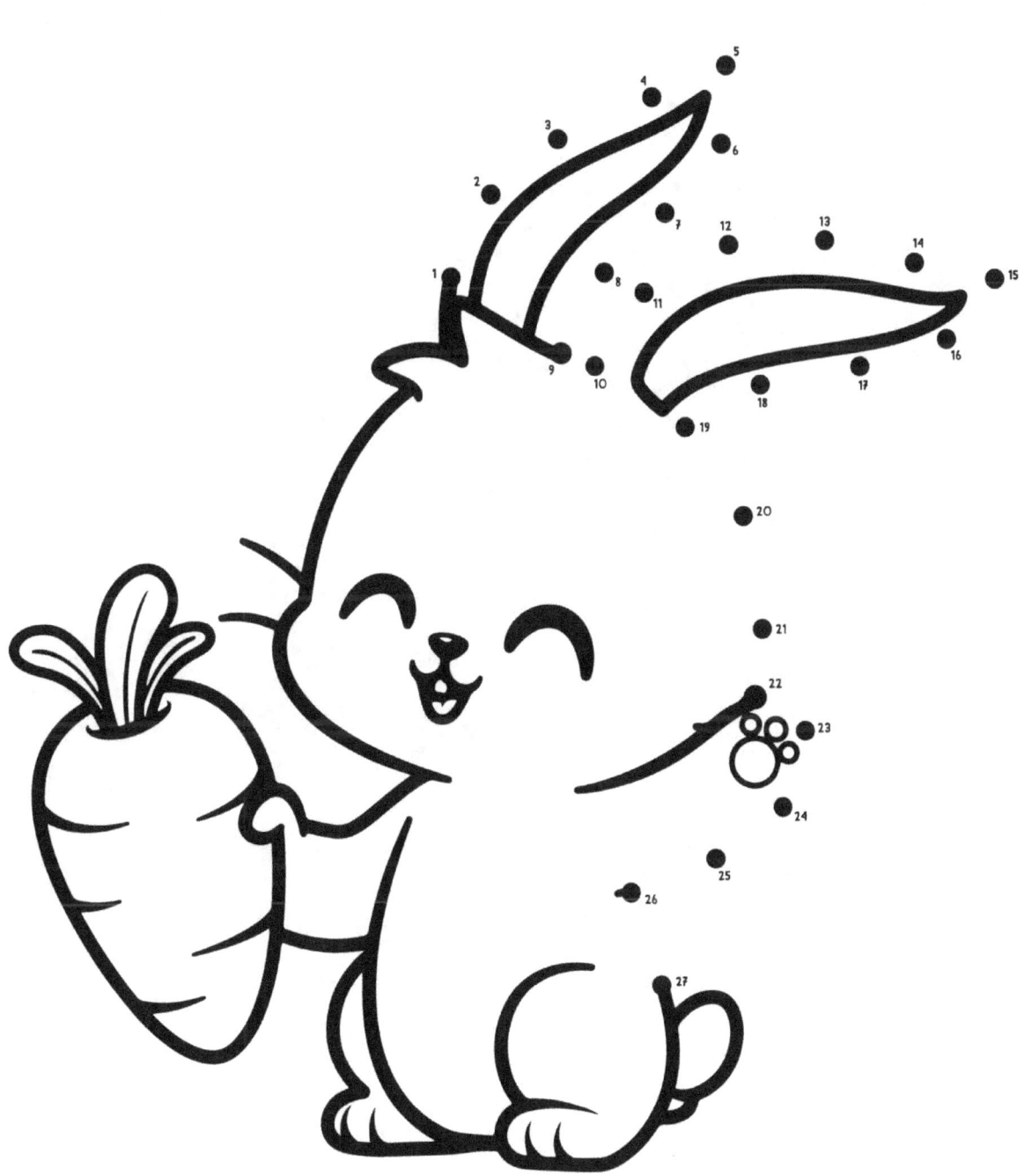

+ Connect The Dots With Numbers
+ Color The Picture Brightly

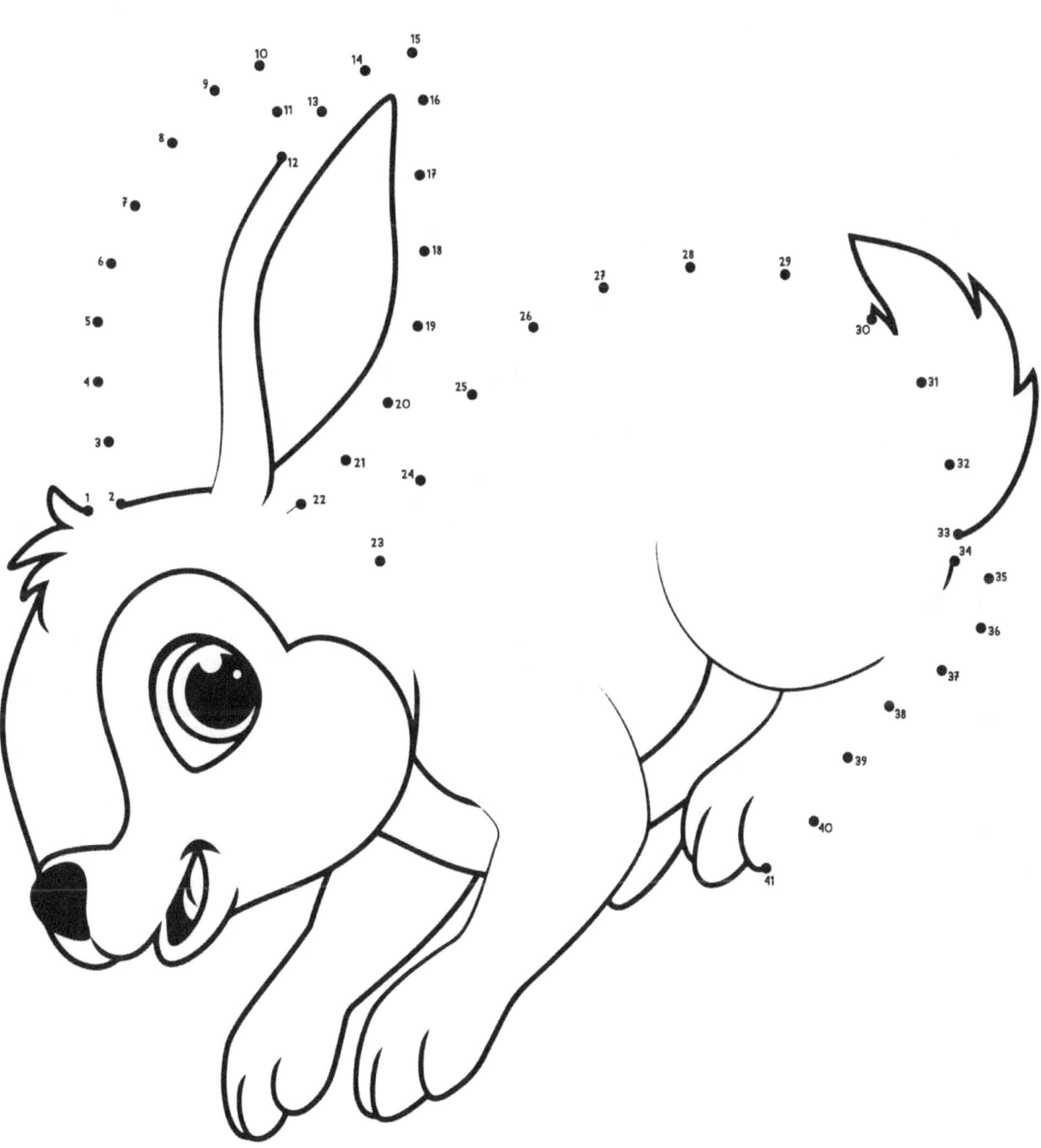

Name:...........................

+ Connect The Dots With Numbers
+ Color The Picture Brightly

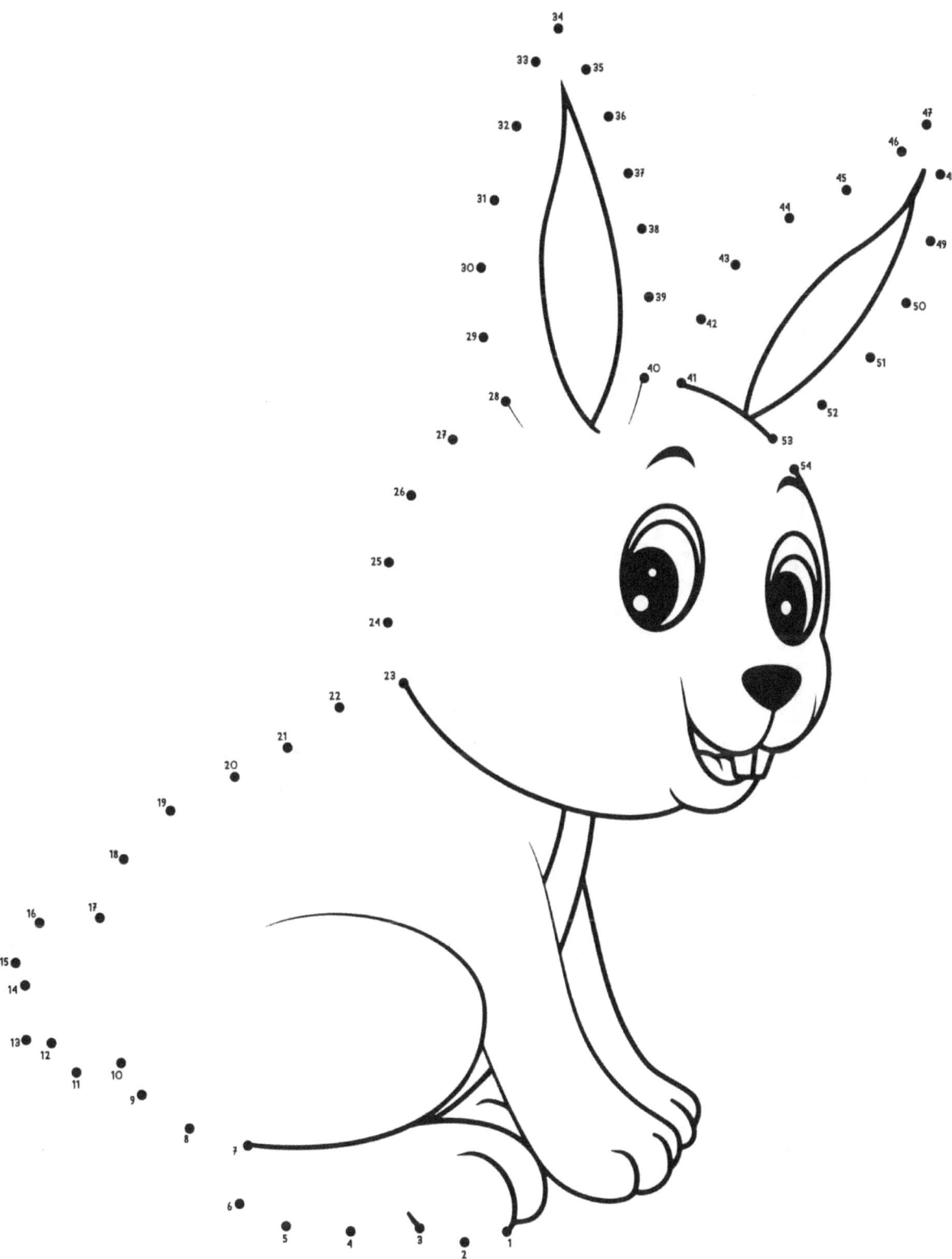

Name:............................

+ Connect The Dots With Numbers
+ Color The Picture Brightly

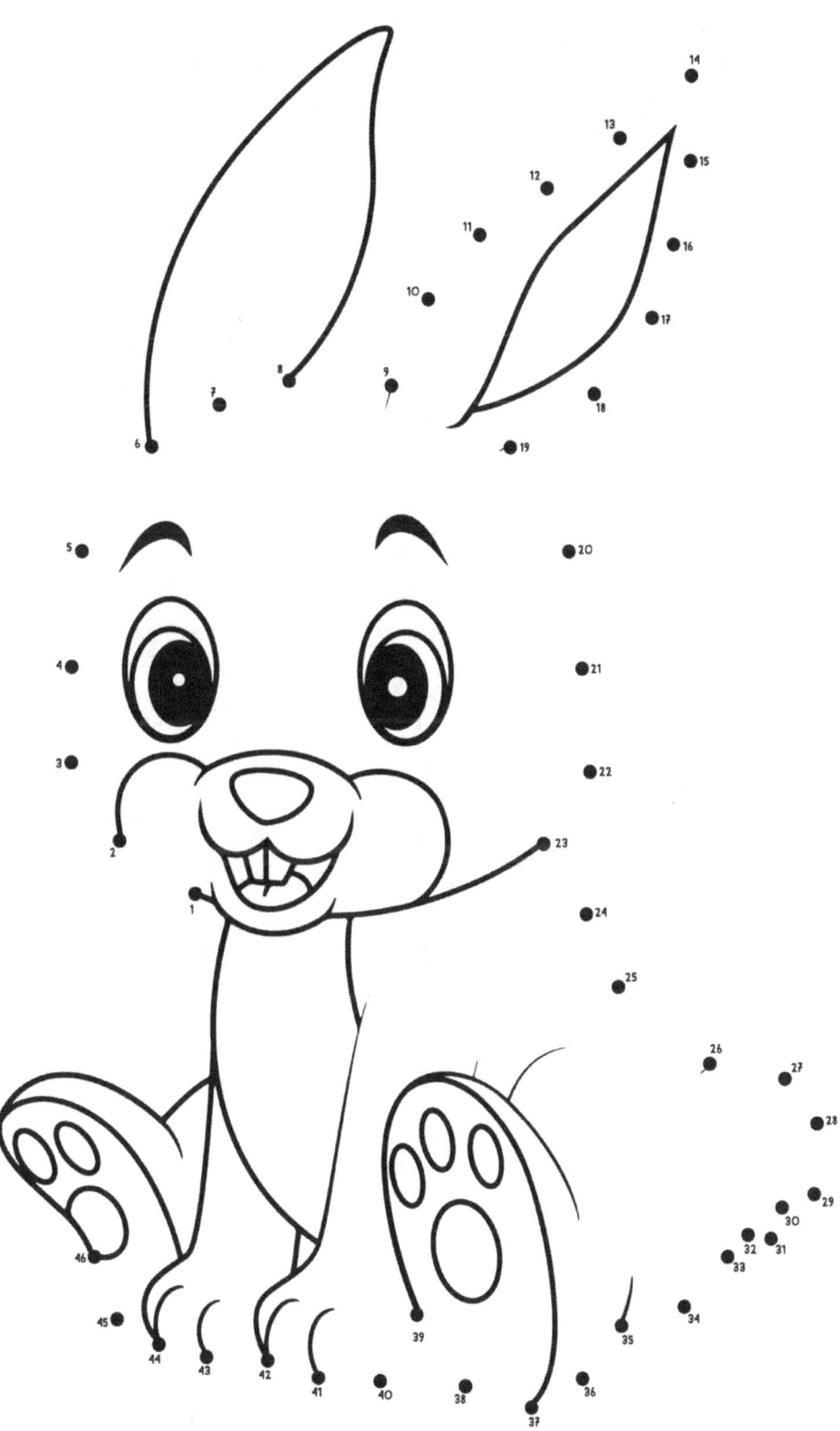

+ Connect The Dots With Numbers
+ Color The Picture Brightly

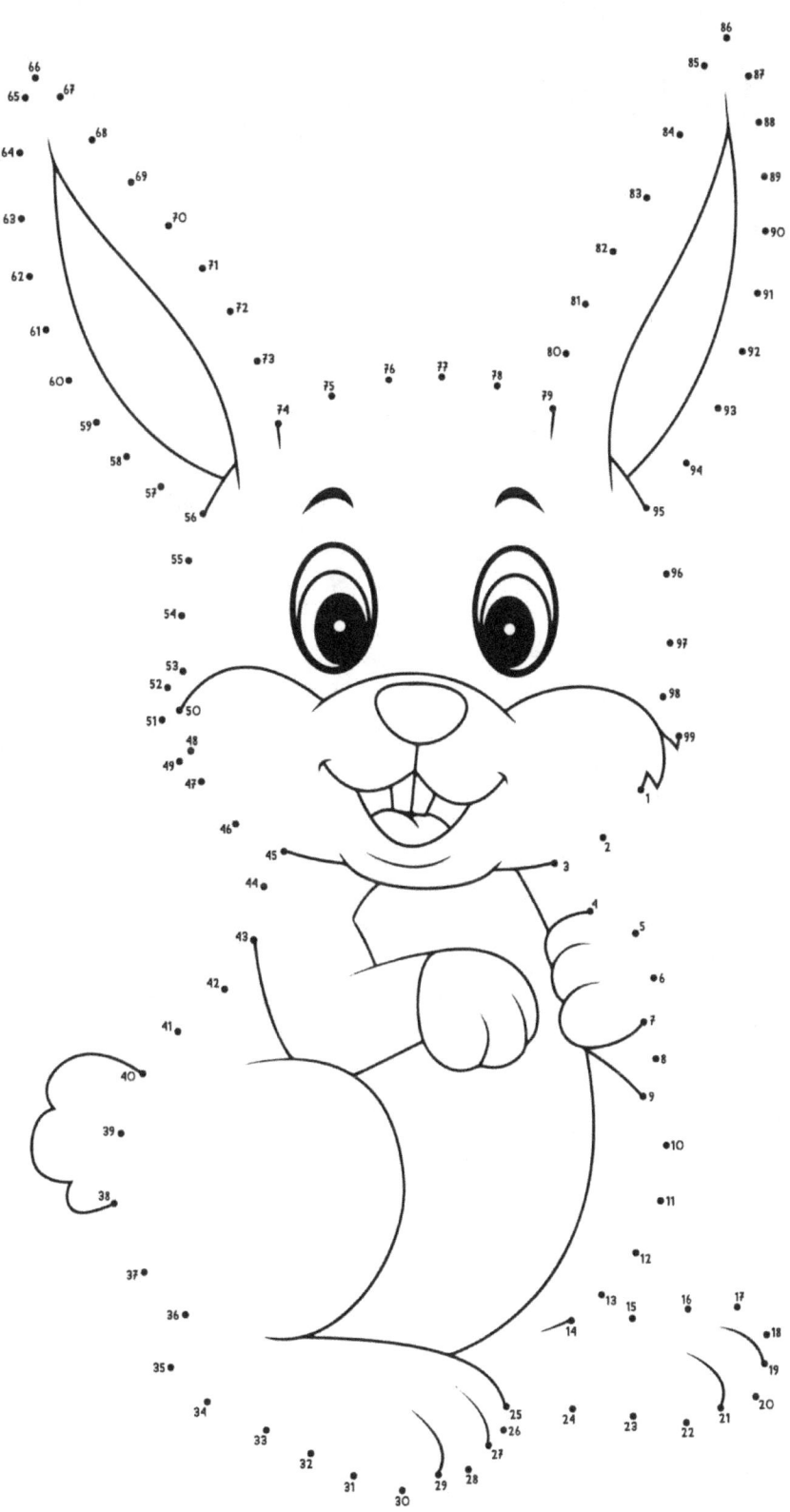

Name:........................

+ Connect The Dots With Numbers
+ Color The Picture Brightly

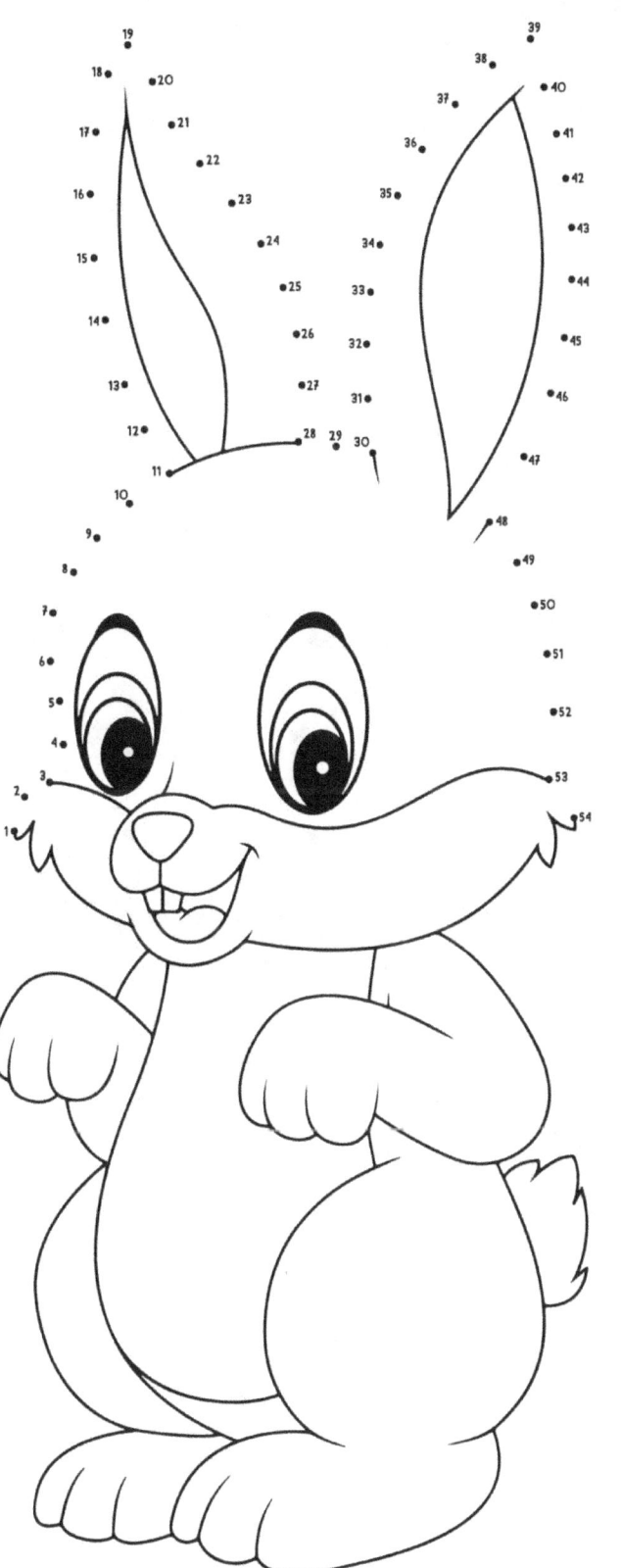

Name:.............................
+ **Connect The Dots With Numbers**
+ **Color The Picture Brightly**

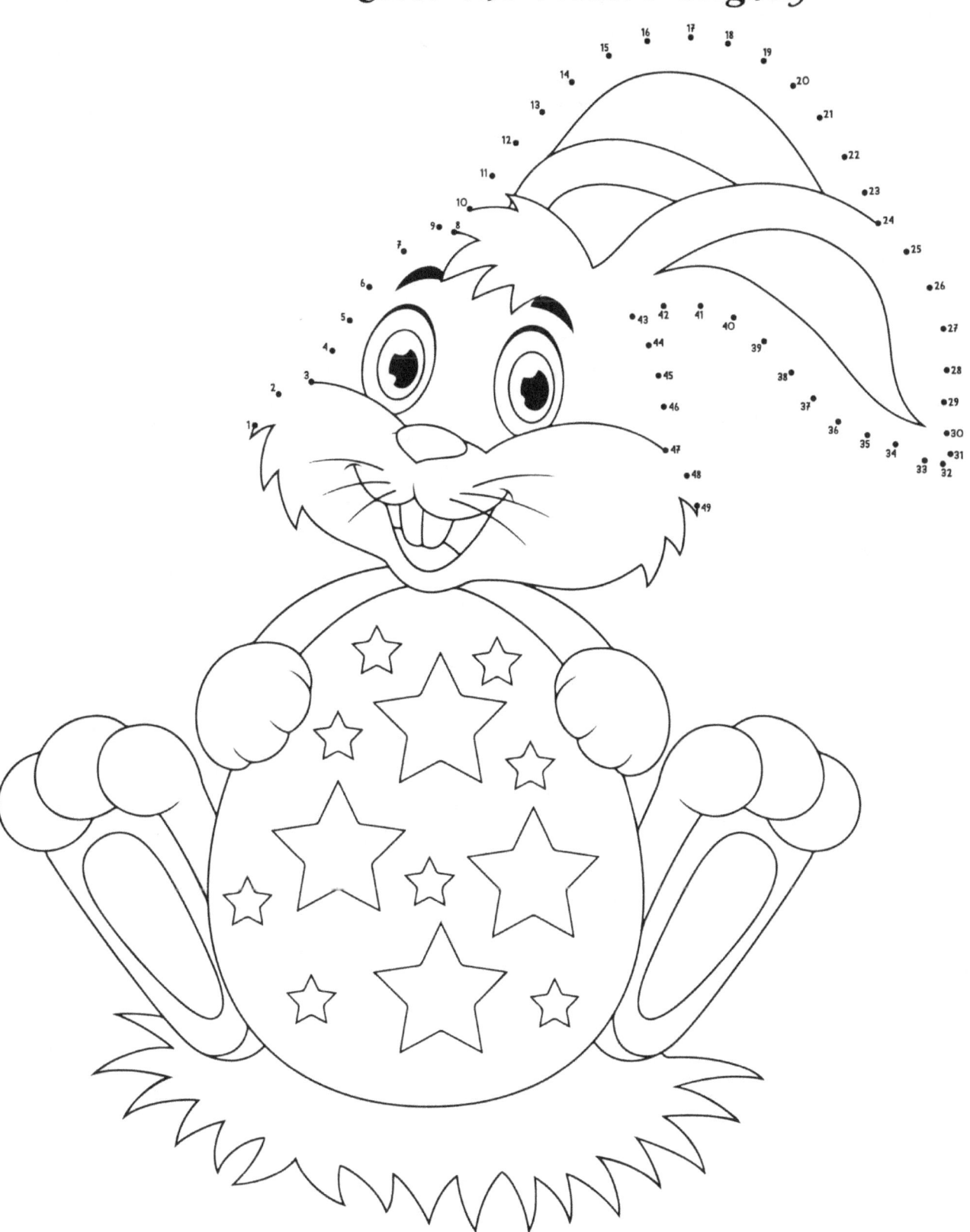

+ Connect The Dots With Numbers
+ Color The Picture Brightly

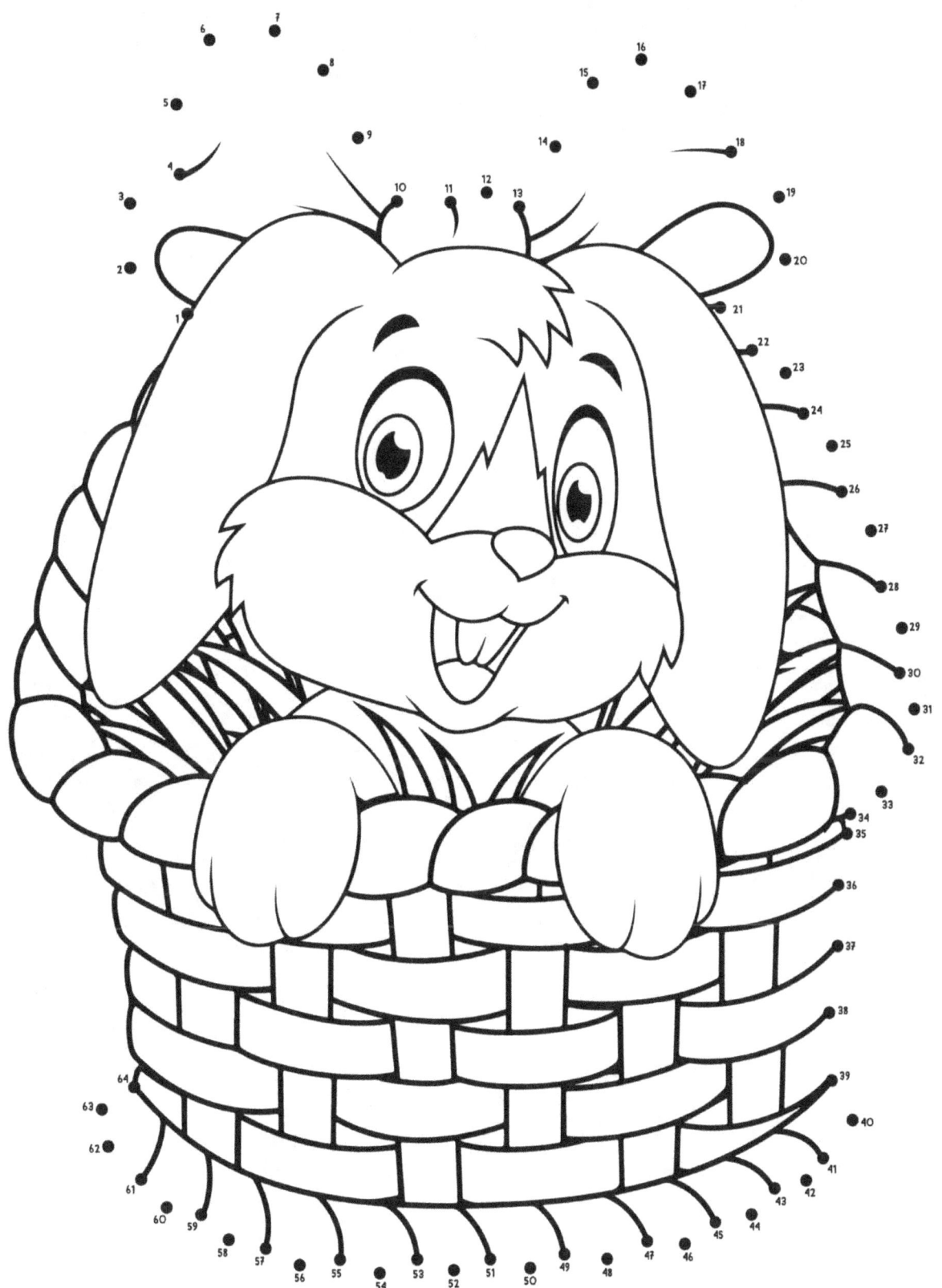

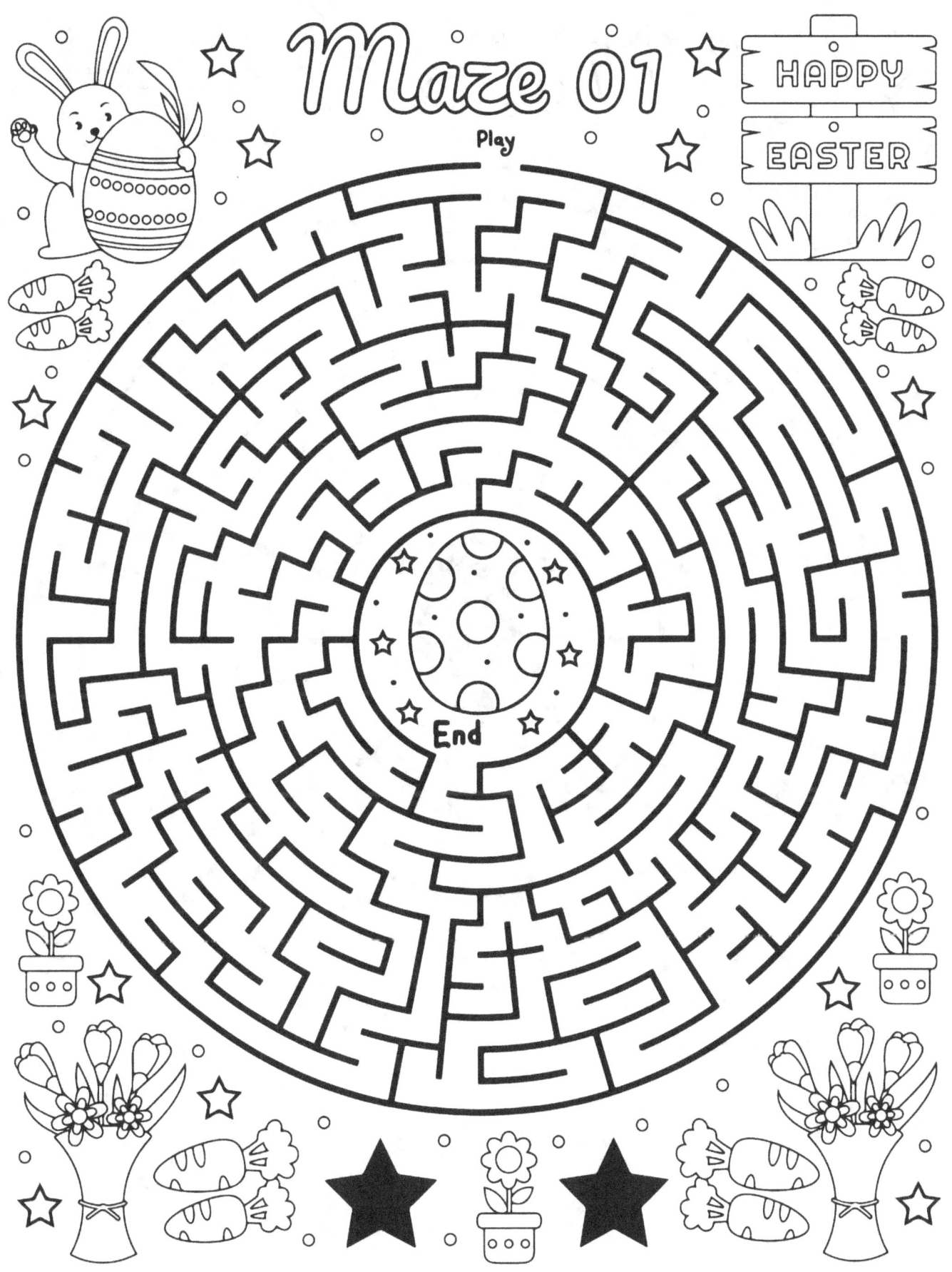

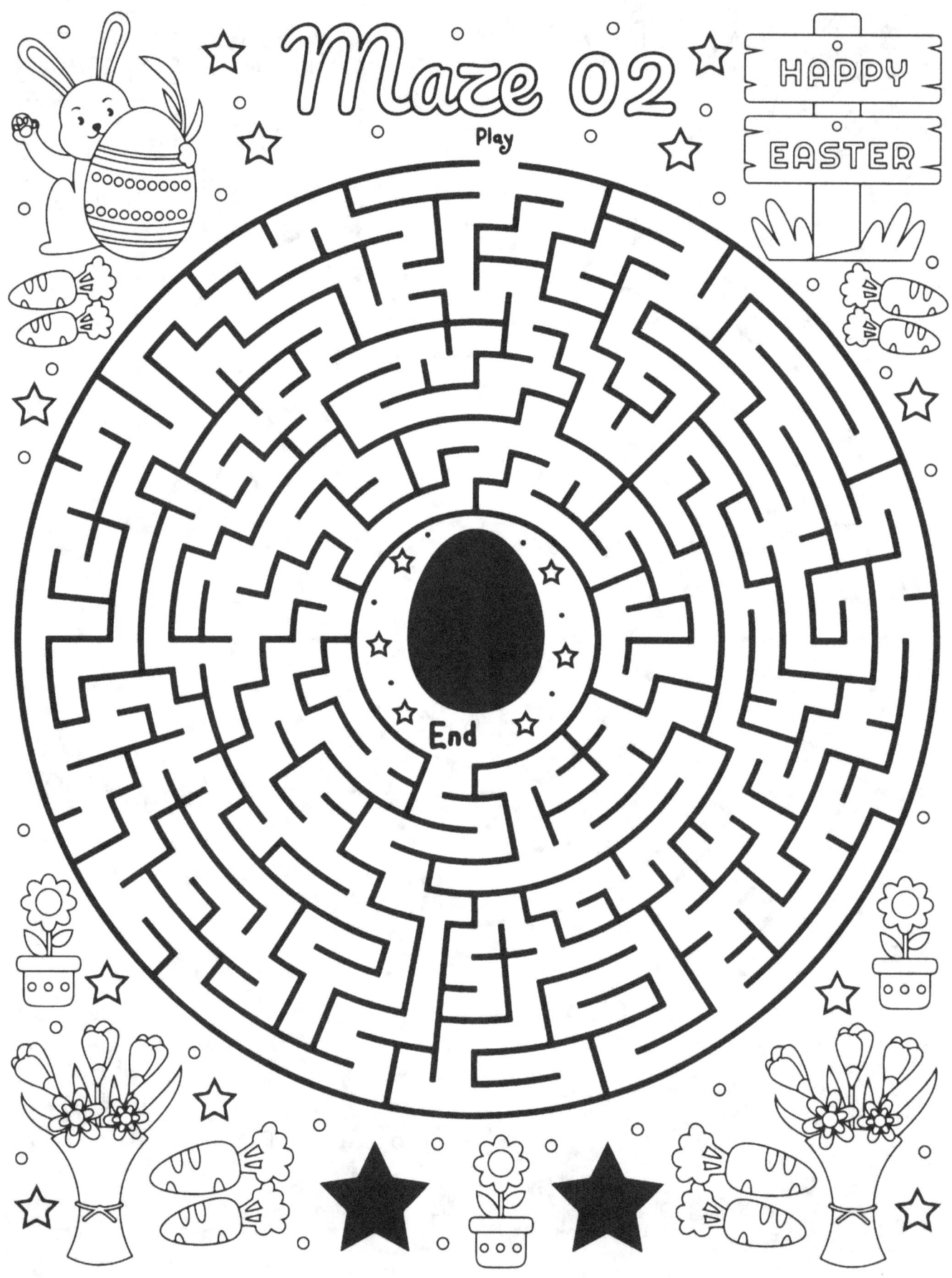

Maze 02

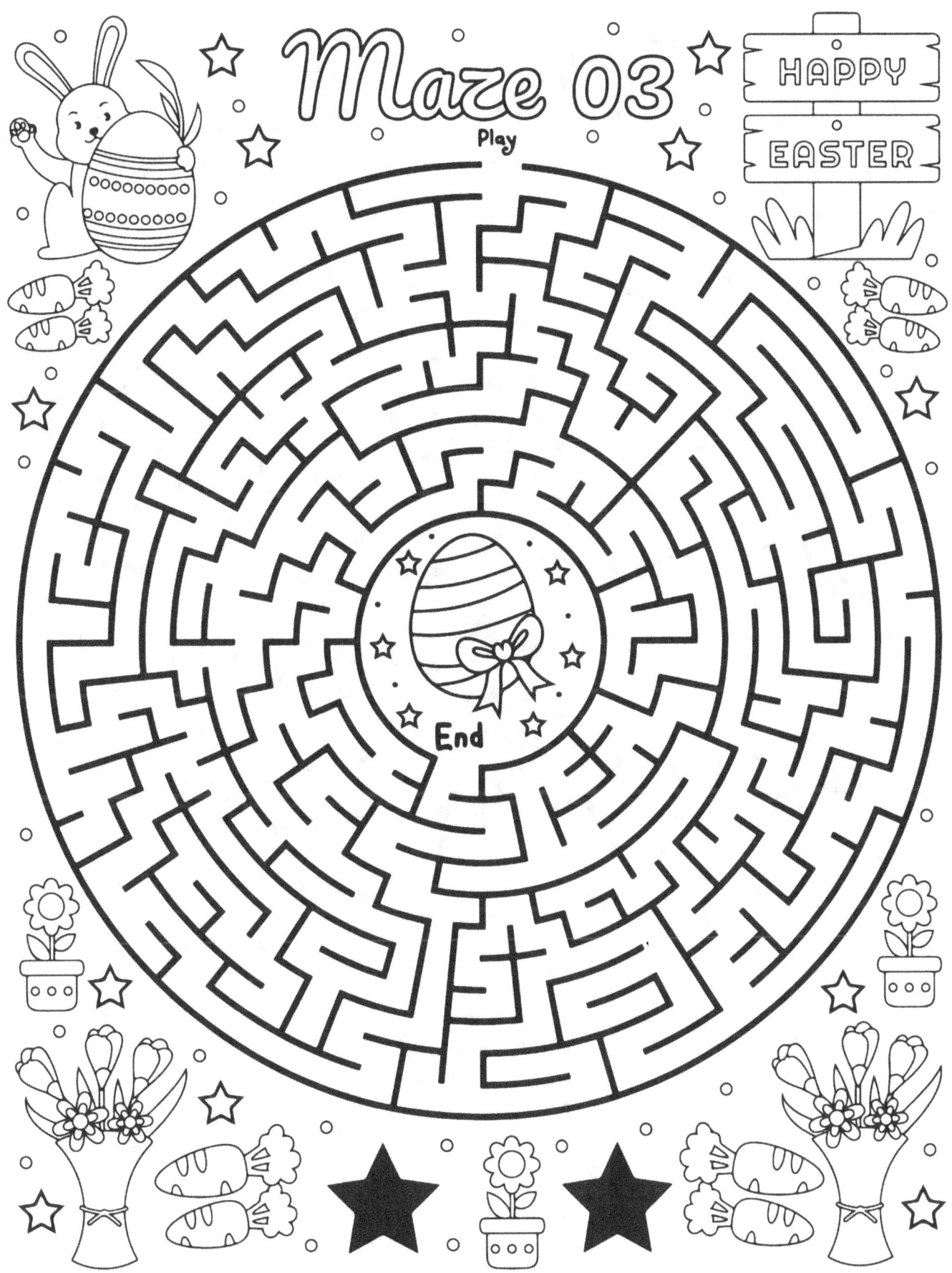

Maze 04

Play

End

HAPPY EASTER

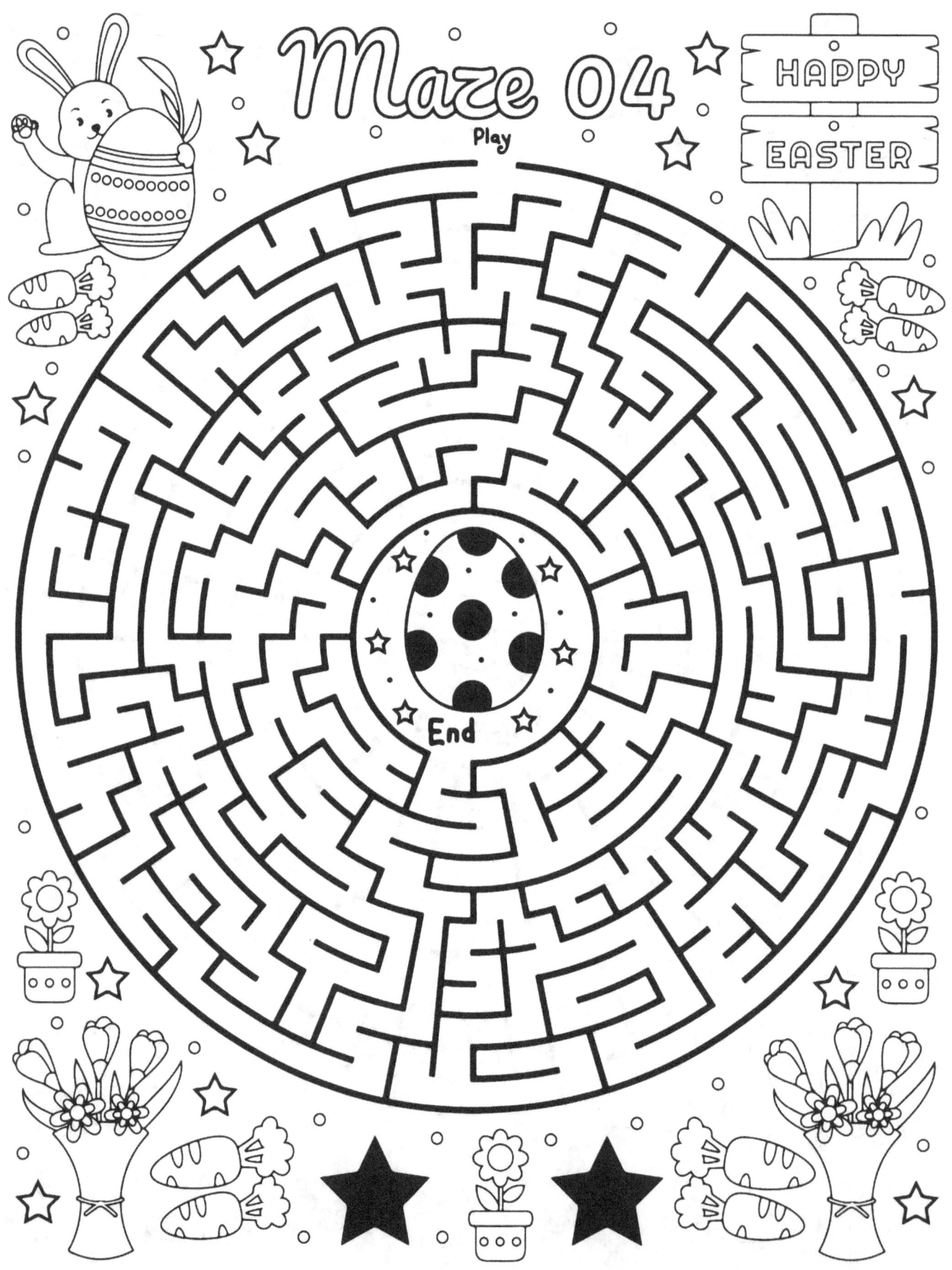

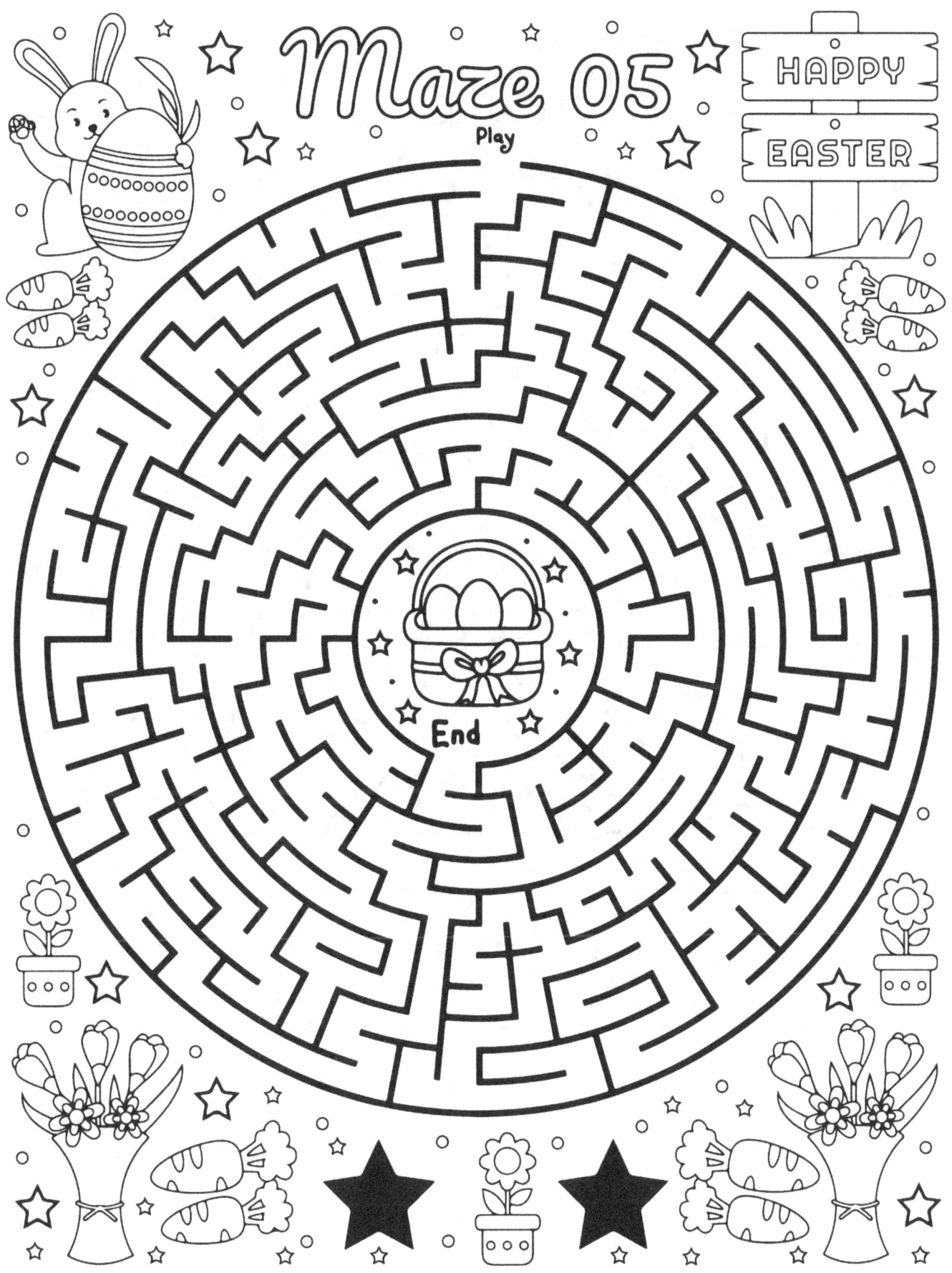

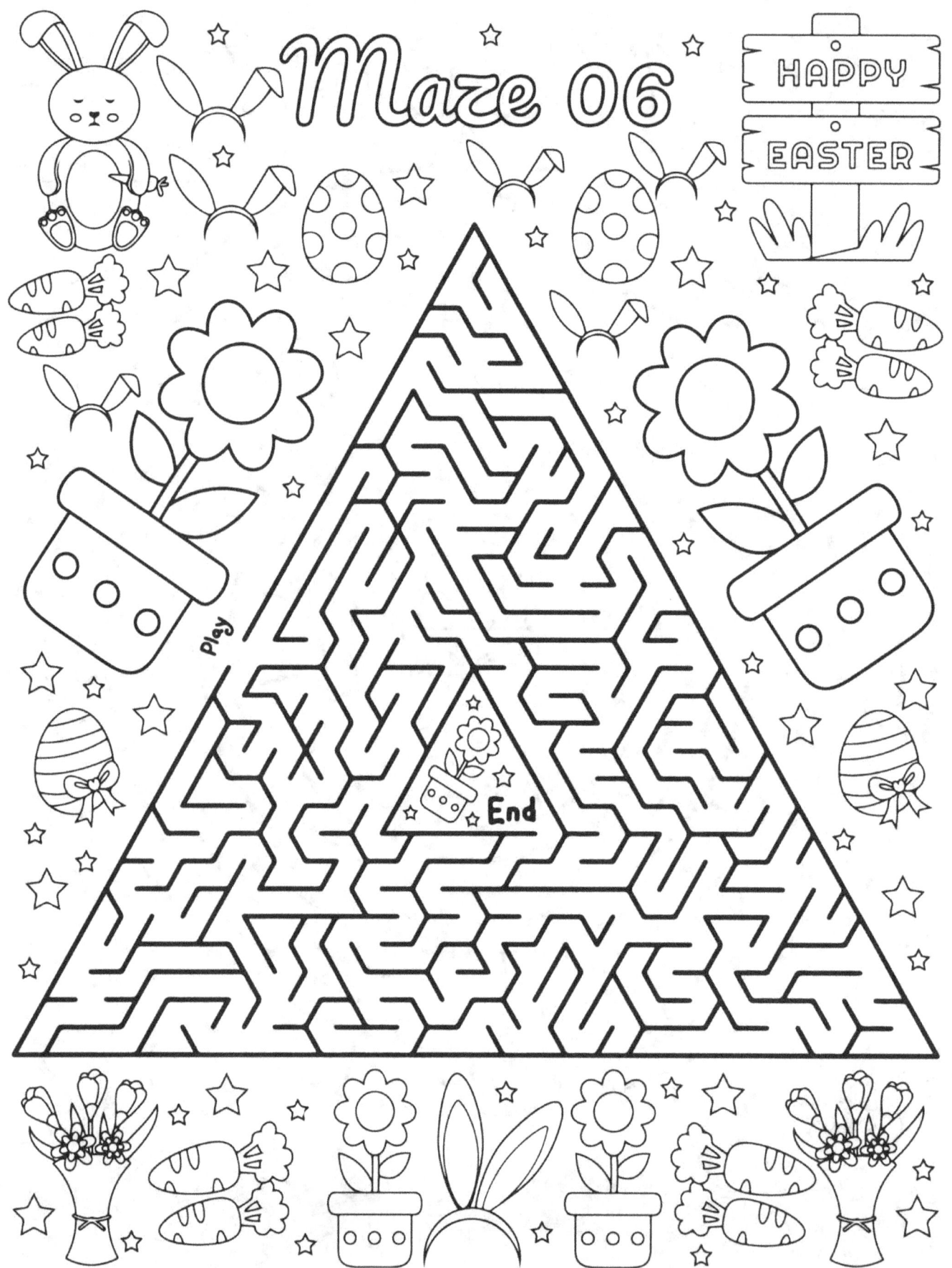

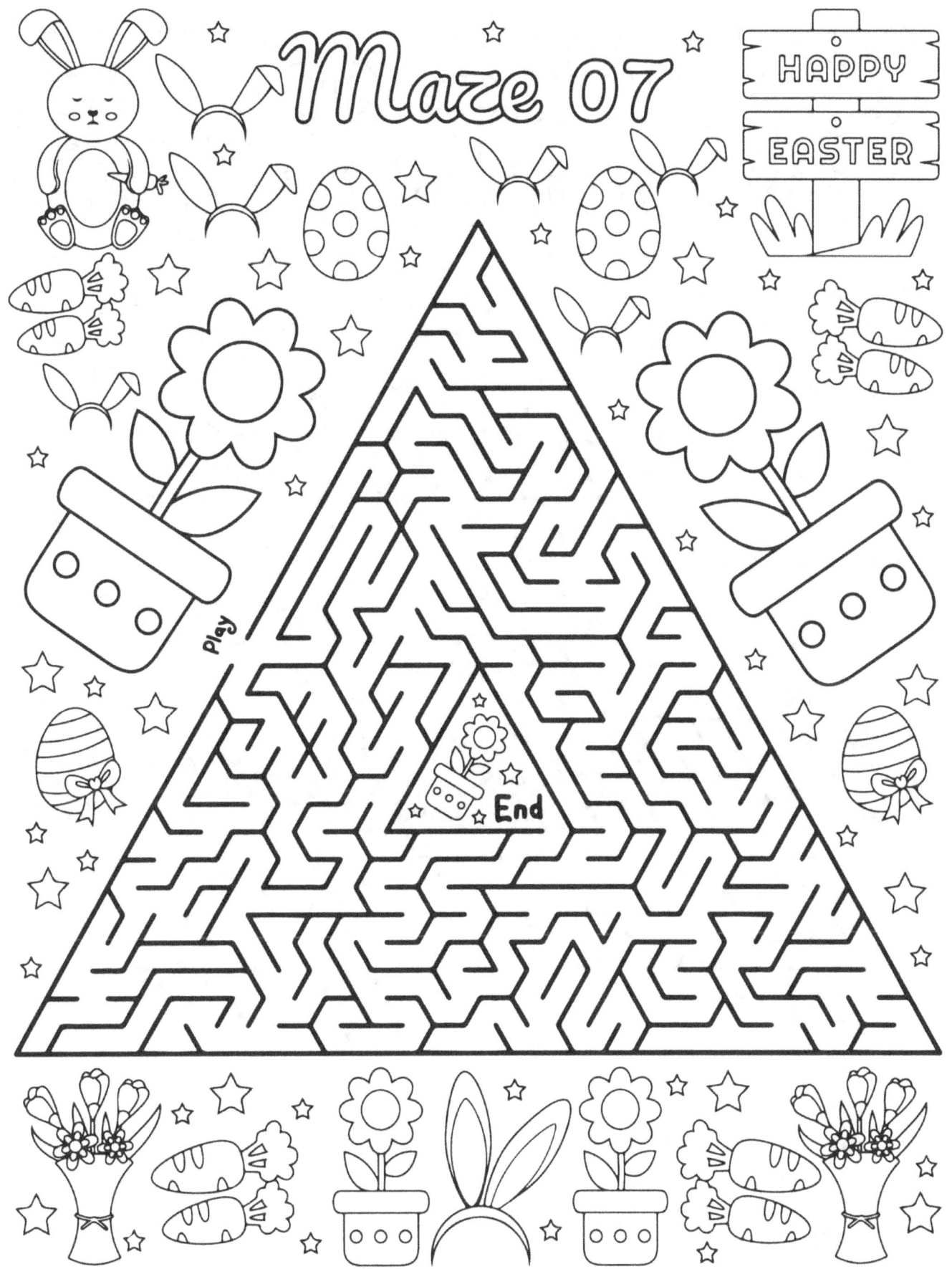

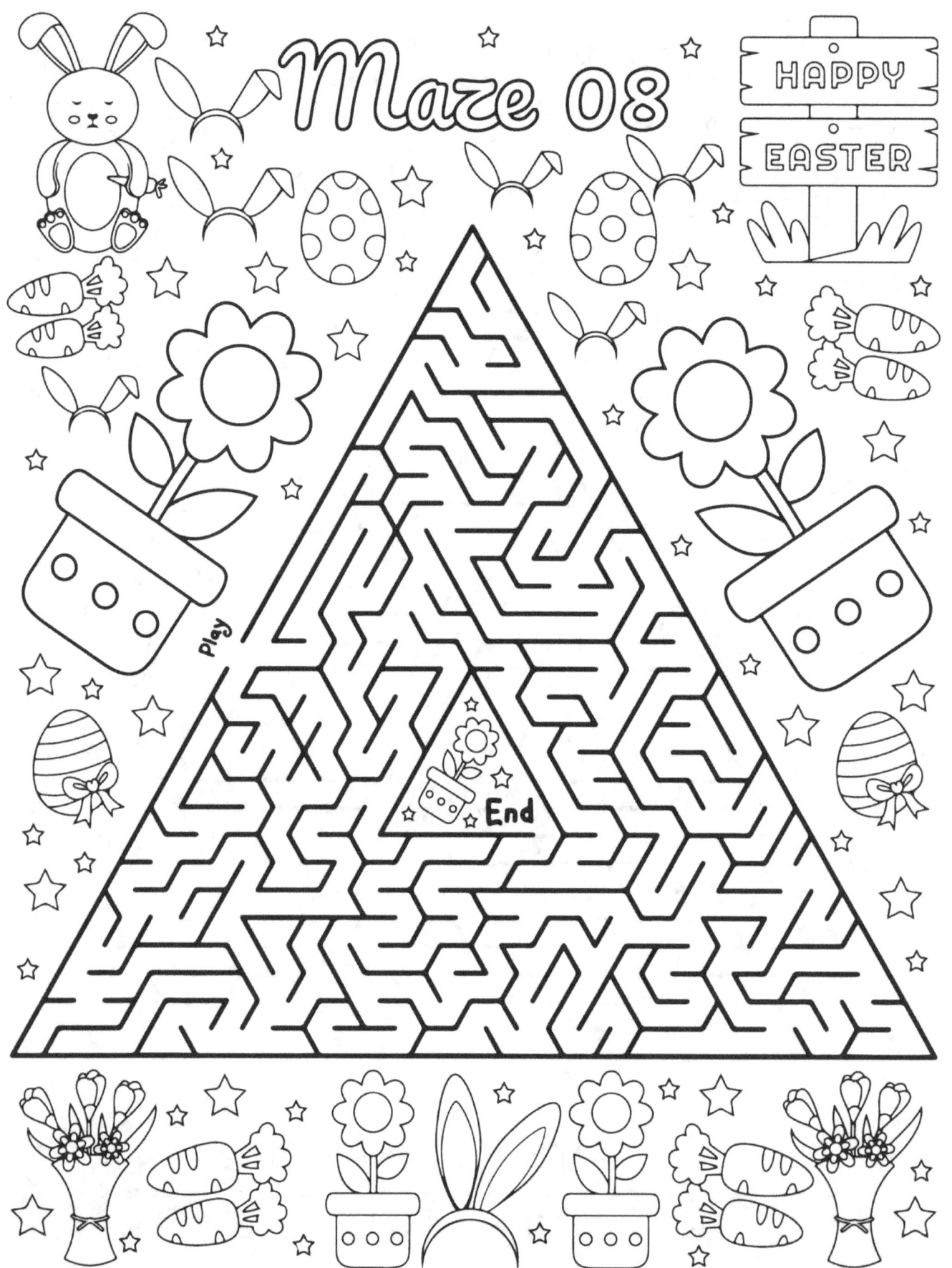

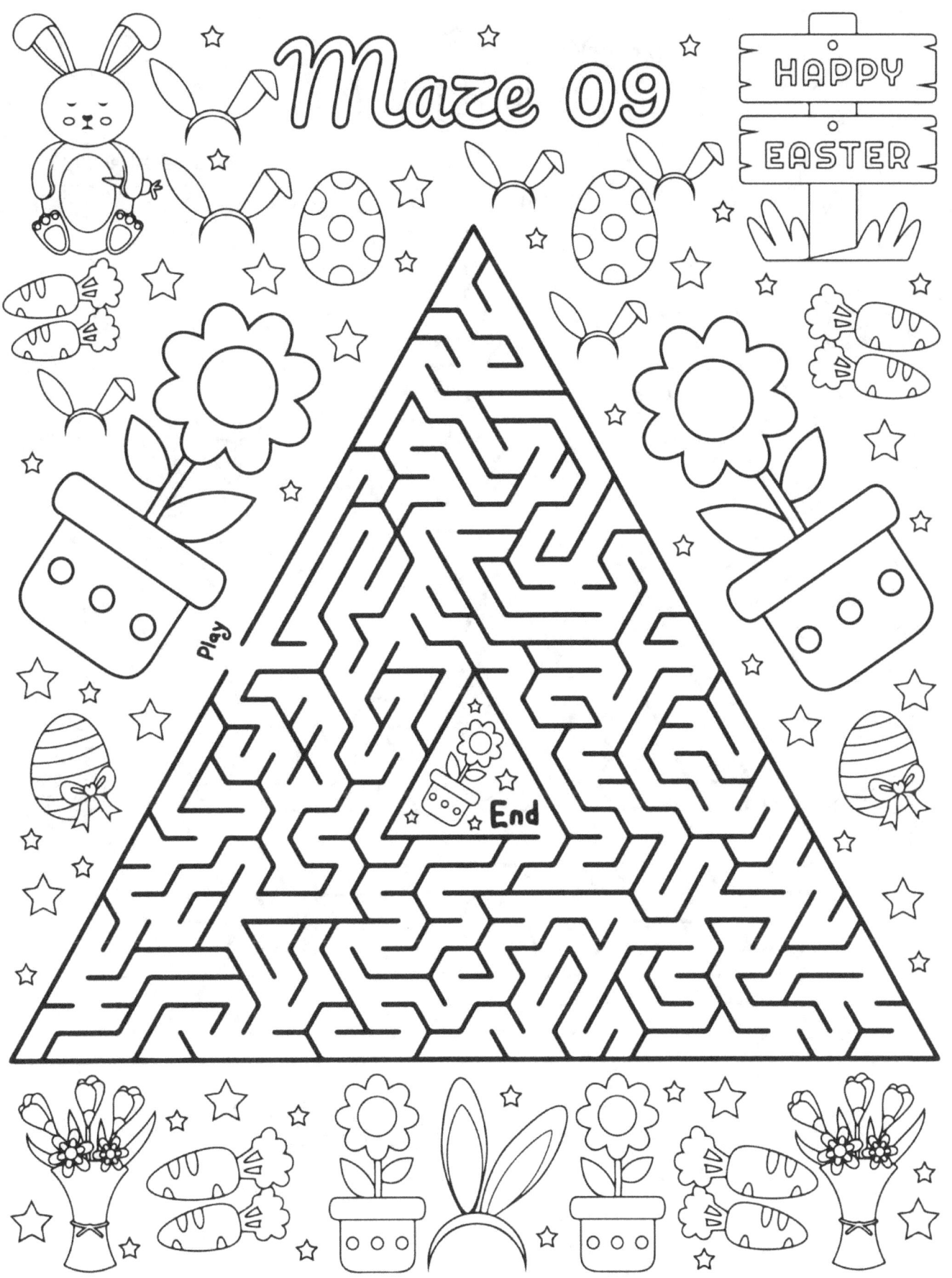

Maze 09

HAPPY EASTER

Play

End

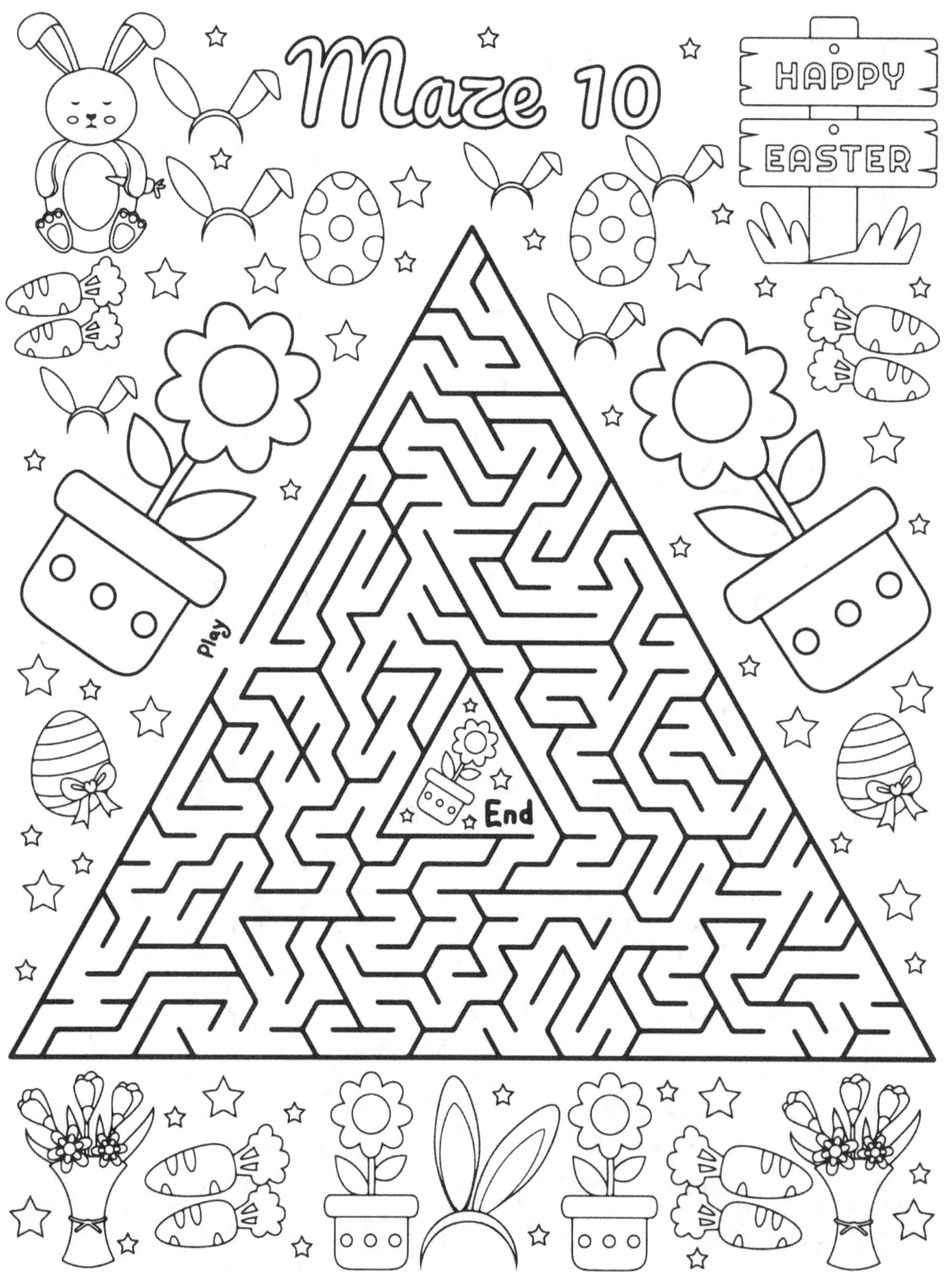

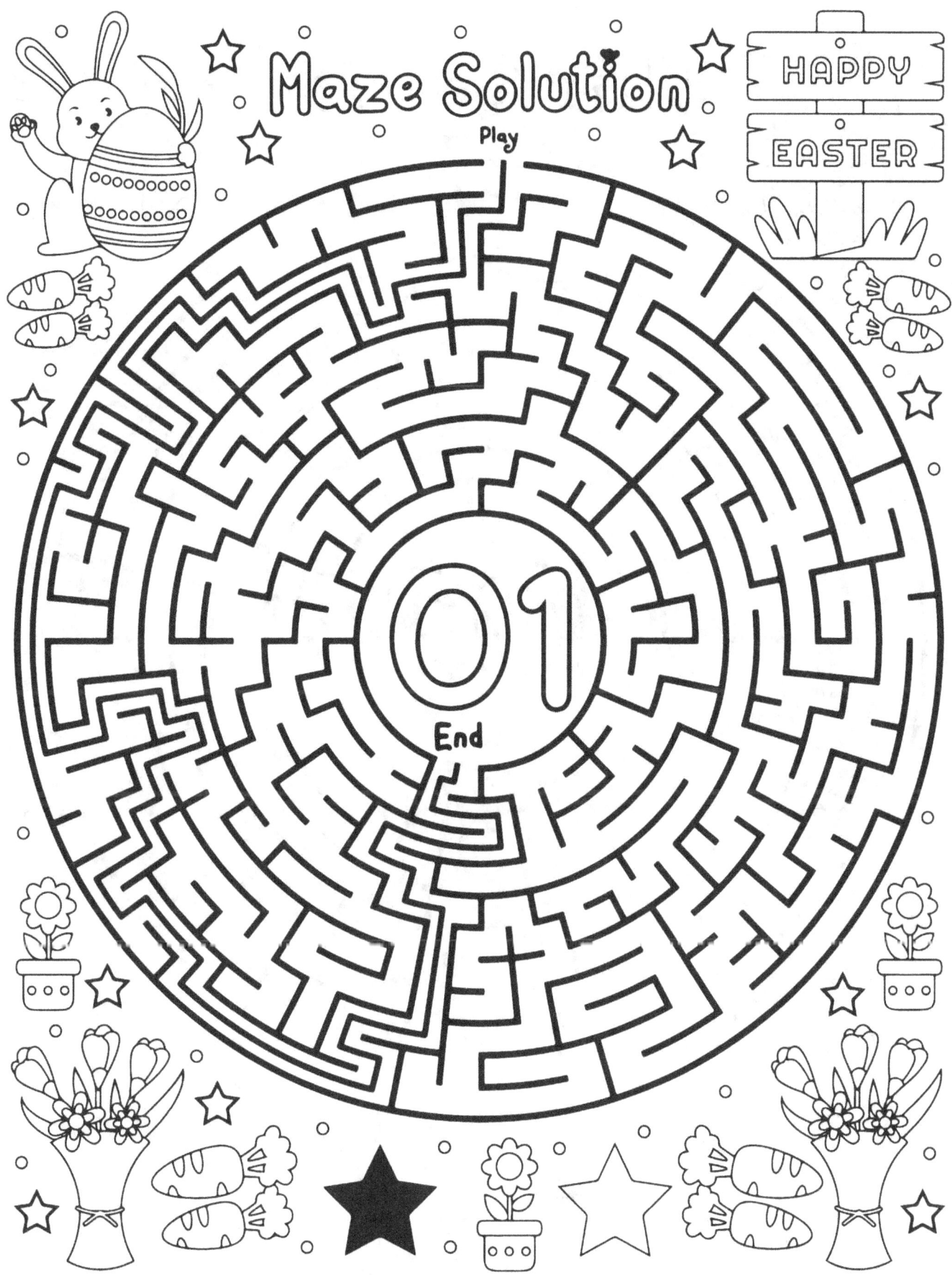

Maze Solution

Play

End

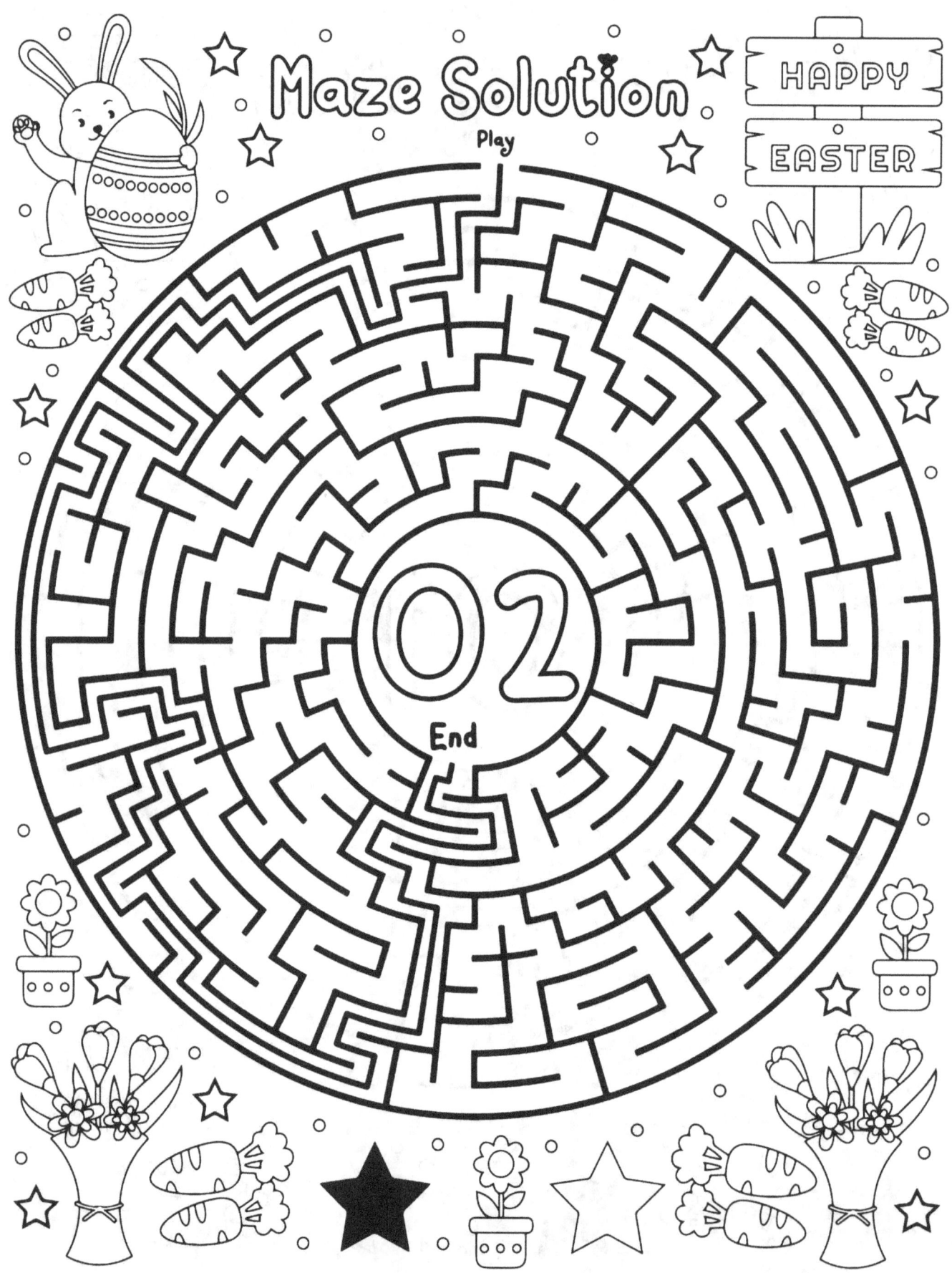

Maze Solution

Play

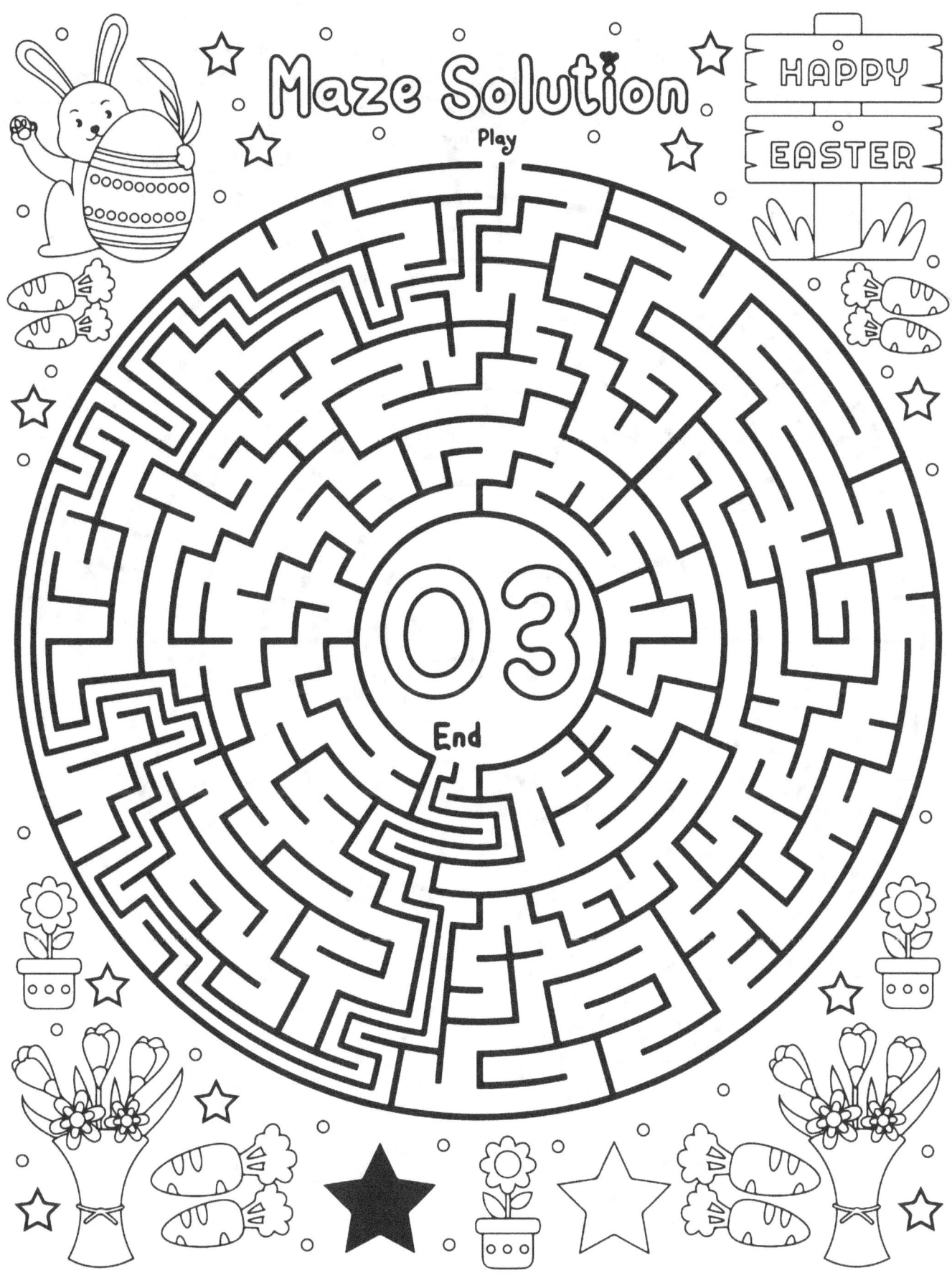

03

End

HAPPY EASTER

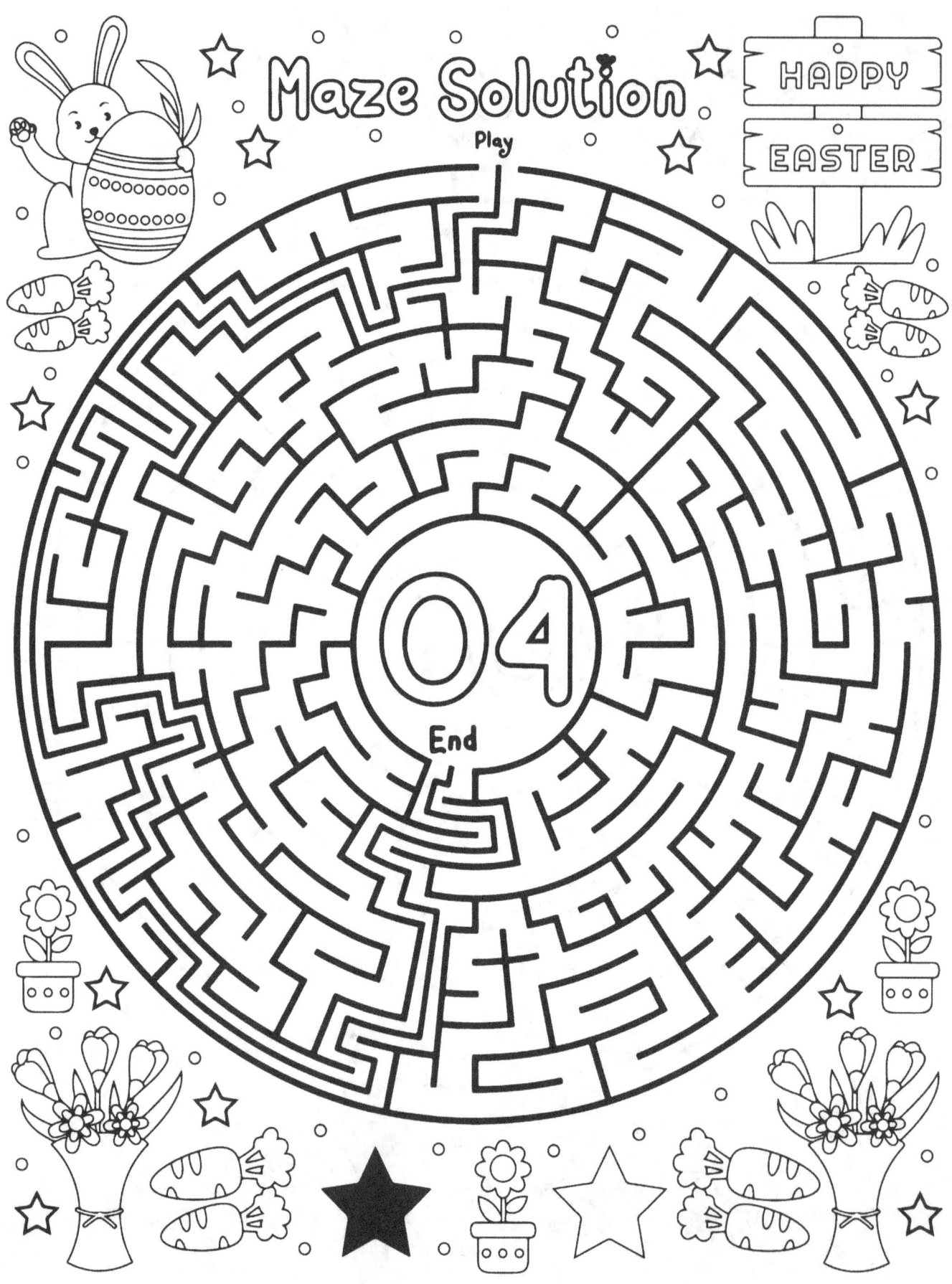

Maze Solution

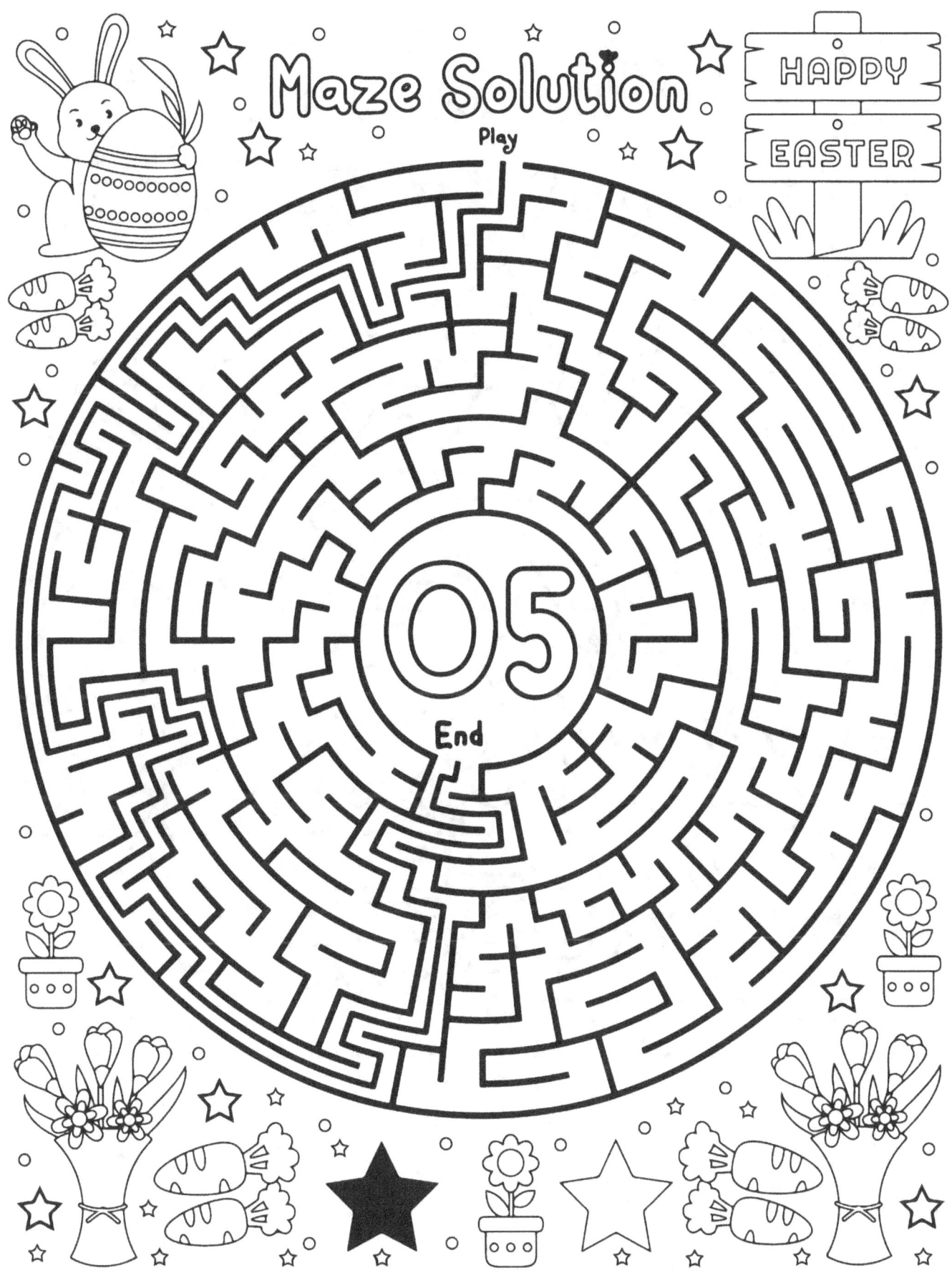

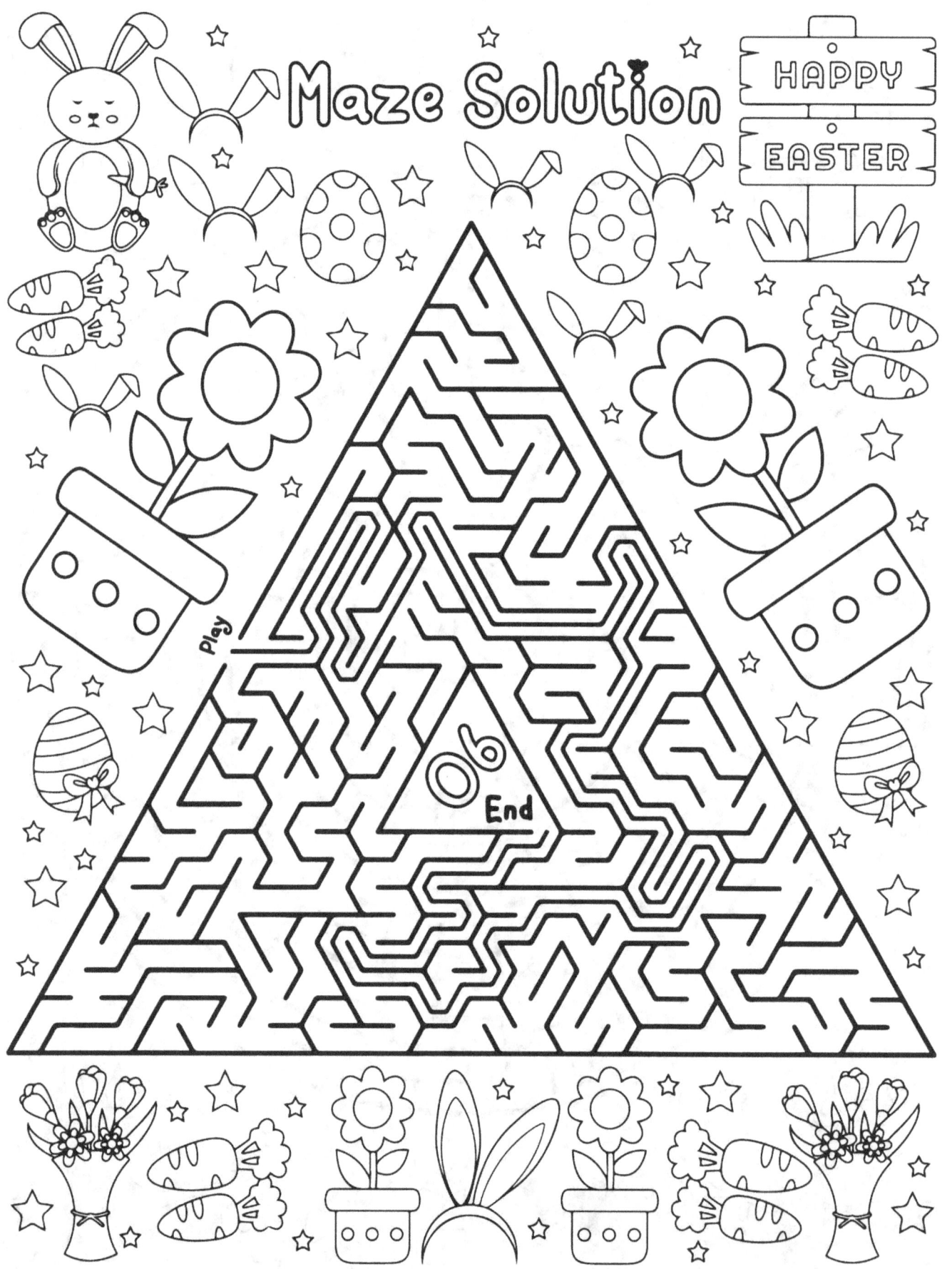

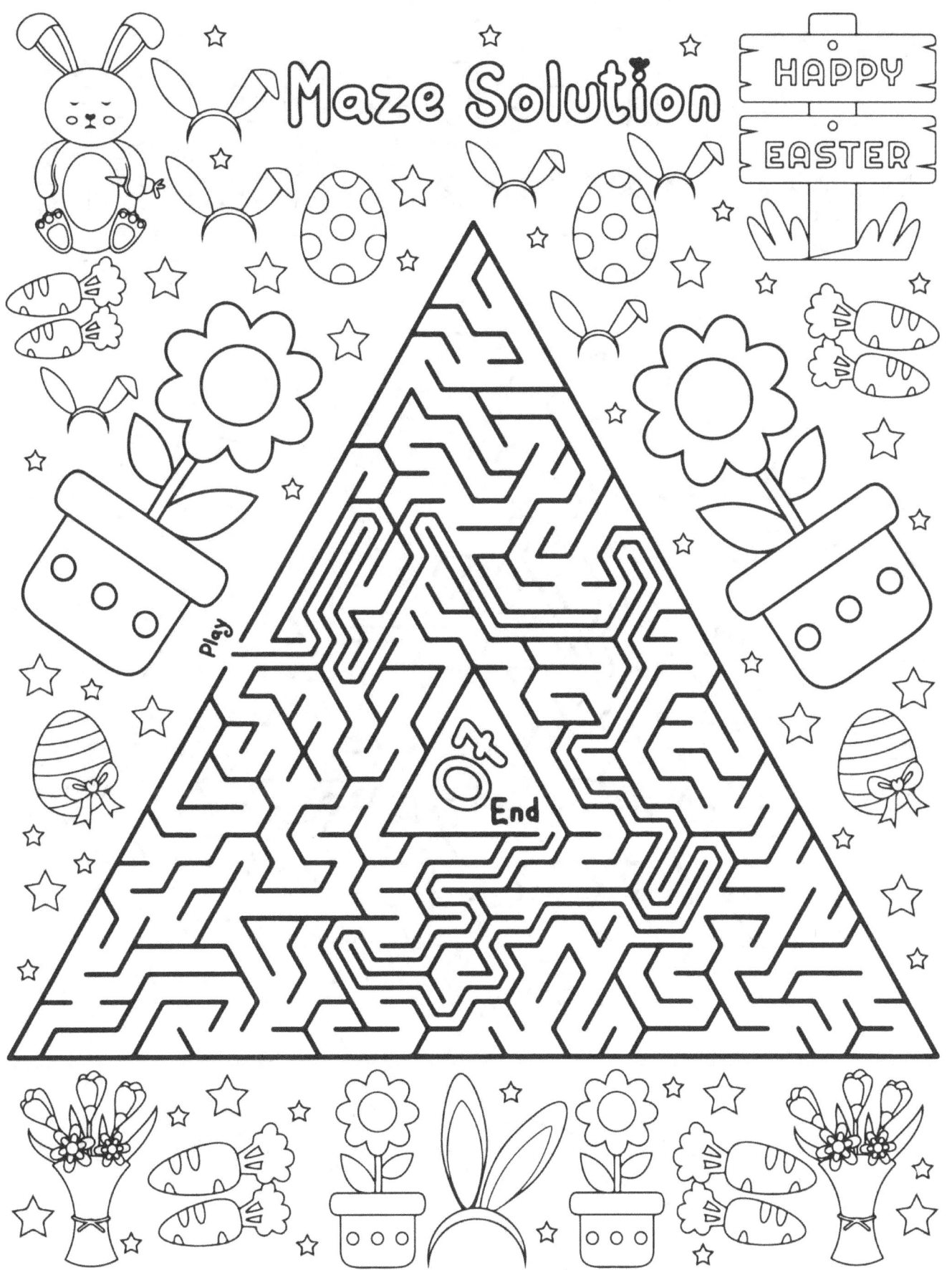

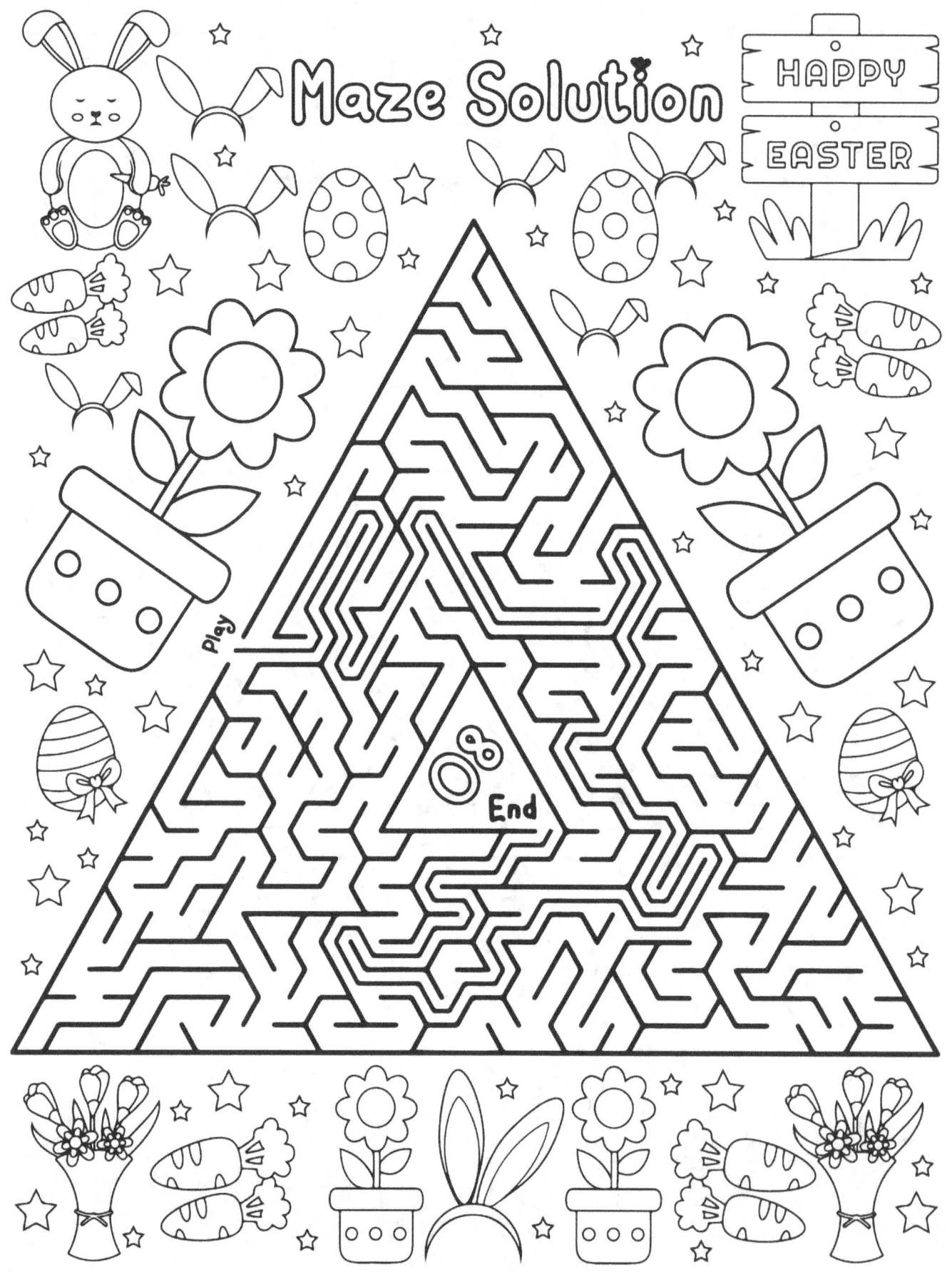

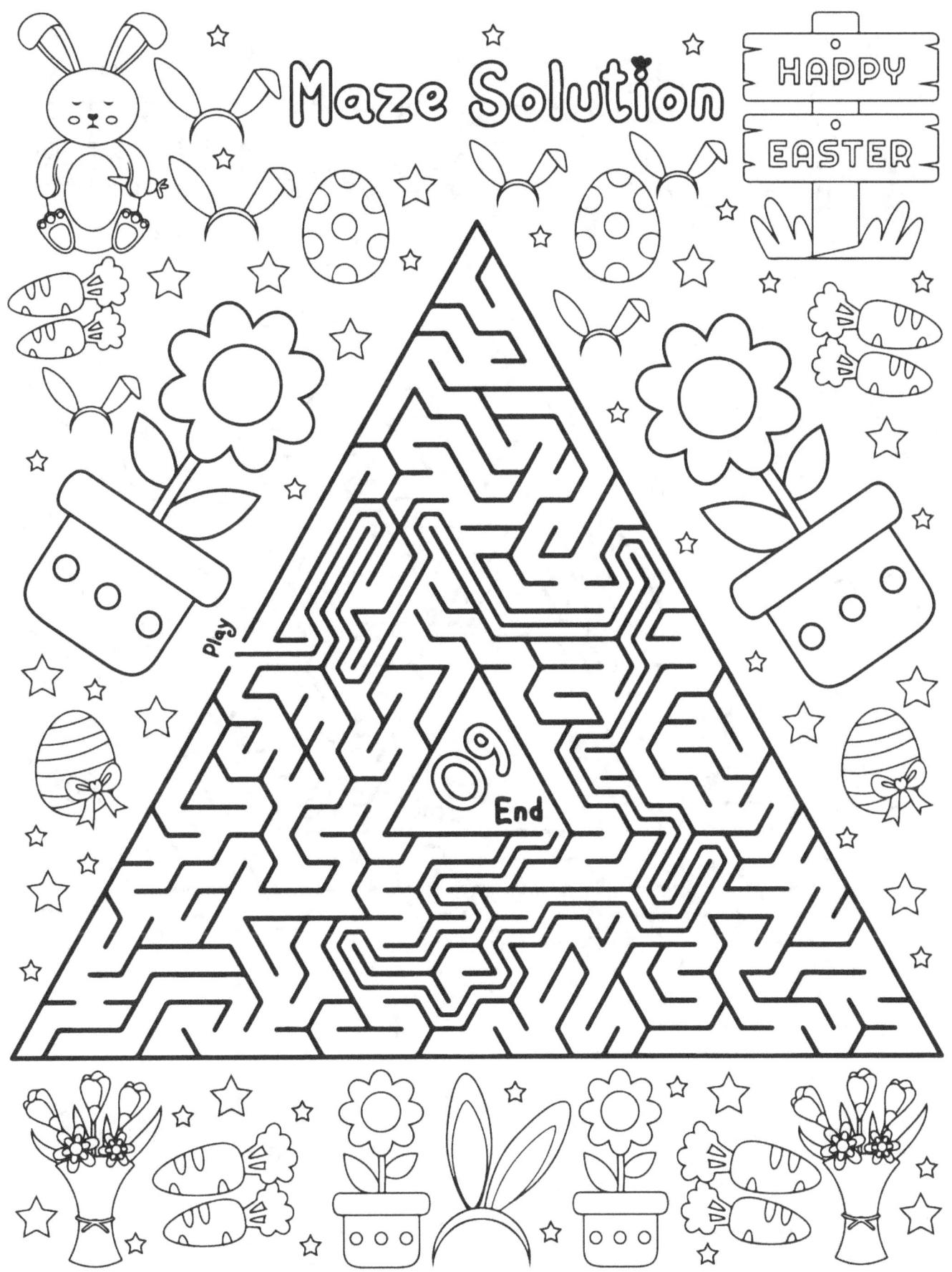

Maze Solution

HAPPY EASTER

Play

End

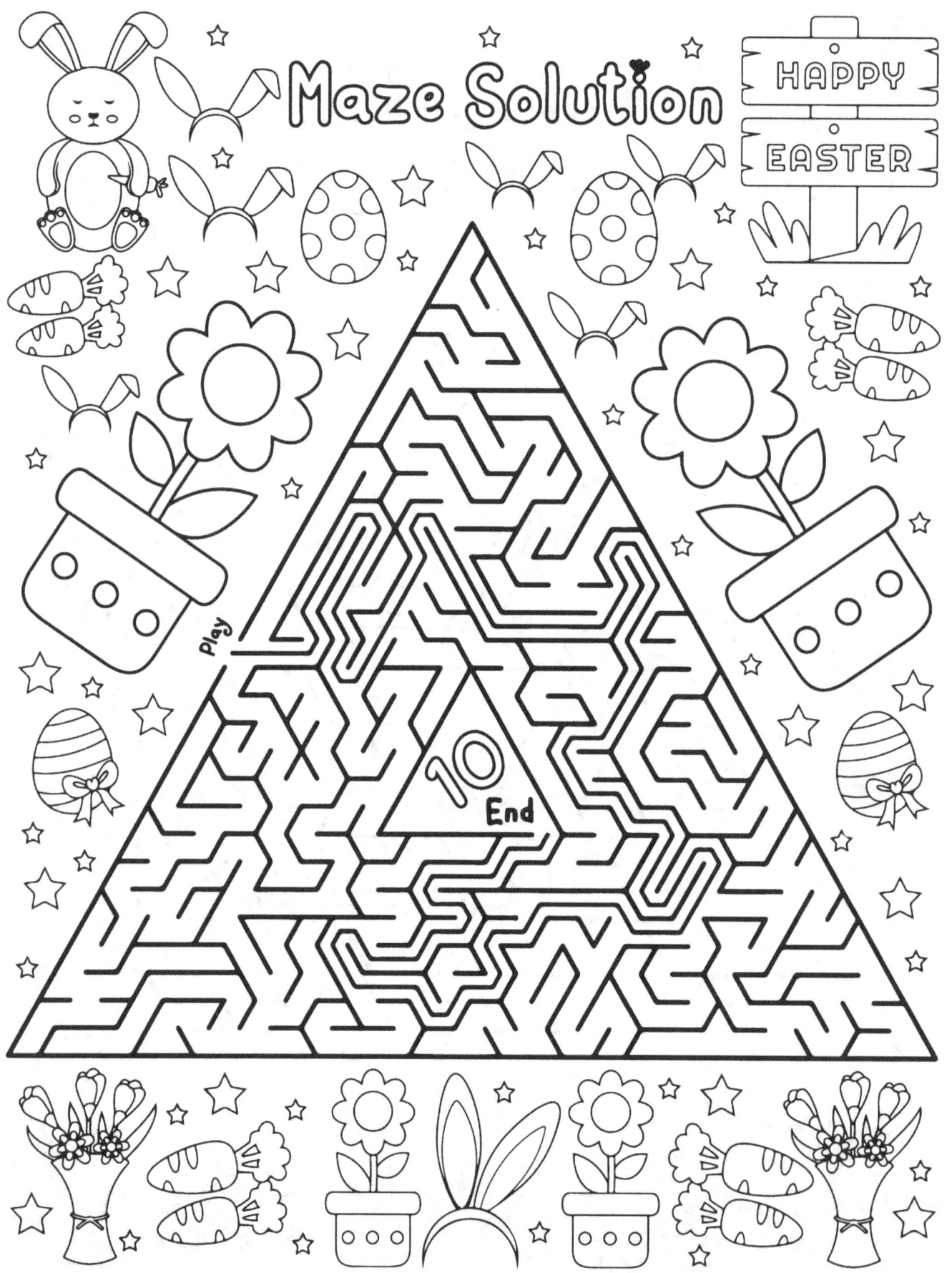

Maze Solution

HAPPY EASTER

Play

10 End

www.ingramcontent.com/pod-product-compliance
Lightning Source LLC
Chambersburg PA
CBHW080915220526
45467CB00030BA/2366